My personal experience reading *When We Were Eve* can be summarized in the following quote. "Our lives are ripe with experiences that both bless and curse us at once, and leave us feeling like strangers who occupy a body that is mostly foreign to us ... You Are Not Alone."

Colleen Mitchell's book contains all the elements a women›s book club craves—a walk through the Scriptures, engaging storytelling, and thoughtful questions to ponder. Her story is personal and vulnerable yet her experiences are universal. Every woman reading *When We Were Eve* will eventually recognize herself within its pages.

As if Colleen's story was not gripping enough, she has assembled an incredible group of women who bear their hearts and reaffirm Colleen›s ascertain that we are truly not alone. I found myself alternating from nodding in emphatic agreement to wiping away tears as if I were my deepest wounds being gently exposed. When I turned the last page and closed *When We Were Eve*, those wounds felt mended and my heart on a new path of healing."

—Allison Gingras, www.ReconciledToYou.com

"I want to get a copy of this book for every woman I know. We're all riddled with insecurities about who we are and what we look like, and Colleen Mitchell has powerful words of wisdom to help us find peace and joy in simply the women God created us to be."

—Jennifer Fulwiler, SiriusXM radio host,
author, *One Beautiful Dream*

Colleen beckons each woman to a contemplation of her integrated self, summoning her to incarnate the glory of a woman's flesh with her fully resurrected soul.

—Sonja Corbitt, the Bible Study Evangelista, author of
Unleashed, Fearless, Ignite, and *Fulfilled*

When We Were Eve: Uncovering the Woman God Made You to Be by Colleen C. Mitchell is a rich and grace-filled book written by a woman whose pen in hand reveals a body and soul in love with God. "Our bodies must pursue holiness," Colleen reminds all of us. Colleen's writing talent is a true gift of the Lord to all readers, but especially to we women. As you read, your feminine heart will see God's image in your body and your spirit. Then Colleen shows us, in her reflections and the collected stories from women who strive for sanctity, just exactly how to use our spirituality and our bodily experiences to seek our God. You will "find [yourself]...embracing womanhood without shame!" By the end of this read, you will revel in His great Mercy, bringing you back to Eden in the Sacraments of Holy Mother Church, the Bride of Christ!

—Carol Younger, author, *33 Days to Morning Glory Retreat Companion,* contributing author, *Walk in Her Sandals*

WHEN WE WERE EVE

[
UNCOVERING THE WOMAN
GOD CREATED YOU TO BE
]

COLLEEN C. MITCHELL

franciscan
media
Cincinnati, Ohio

Scripture passages have been taken from *New Revised Standard Version Bible*, copyright ©1989 by the Division of Christian Education of the National Council of the Churches of Christ in the U.S.A., and used by permission. All rights reserved.

Cover design by Mary Ann Smith
Book design by Mark Sullivan

LIBRARY OF CONGRESS CATALOGING-IN-PUBLICATION DATA
Names: Mitchell, Colleen (Catholic Missionary), author.
Title: When we were Eve : uncovering the woman God created you to be / Colleen C. Mitchell.
Description: Cincinnati : Franciscan Media, 2017. | Includes bibliographical references.
Identifiers: LCCN 2017042503 | ISBN 9781632532121 (trade paper)
Subjects: LCSH: Women—Religious aspects—Christianity. | Human body—Religious aspects—Christianity. | Eve (Biblical figure) | Catholic Church—Doctrines.
Classification: LCC BT704 .M58 2017 | DDC 248.8/43--dc23
LC record available at https://lccn.loc.gov/2017042503

ISBN 978-1-63253-212-1

Published by Franciscan Media.
28 W. Liberty St.
Cincinnati, OH 45202
www.FranciscanMedia.org

Printed in the United States of America
Printed on acid-free paper
17 18 19 20 21 5 4 3 2 1

. . . . .

For my men, who teach me continually what the joy of being a woman is about.

For the little cabin in the mountains and its owner, who held me when I couldn't hold myself.

For the woman who walked into my life, parked herself beside me on a garden bench, and never left.

You are love and grace in skin, and you bring me back to myself.

. . . . .

CONTENTS

· · · · ·

INTRODUCTION

The awareness of the meaning of the body…is the fundamental element of human existence in the world.[1]

—JOHN PAUL II

. . . . .

For as long as I can remember, it has seemed to me that my body is a battleground. Because of childhood sexual abuse, the perils of female adolescence, and weight issues, the journey into marriage and sexuality, high-risk pregnancies and unwanted cesarean sections, infant loss and repeated miscarriages, physical and emotional burnout that has led to multiple health concerns—I've felt my body as a liability in one form or another for most of my life.

Yet this body has given itself to me again and again as blessing. It has danced en pointe and given me the gift of making the magic of ballet, has conceived ten babies and gestated six until it birthed them into this world in its own unique way, given itself in the intimate sexual love of marriage over and over again and brought me blushing satisfaction, walked the dirt roads of the ends of the earth with conviction and purpose as a missionary, nursed babies, written meaningful words, swum in the ocean and climbed waterfalls and gazed up at a dark sky lit with a full moon and millions of blinking stars. My body has given me the best parts of my life.

The truth remains that far too many times the trauma of the battle has left me with wounds so deep that the life of blessing fails to eclipse the mistrust I have of this body of mine. When I view my body through spiritual eyes, the same is often true. I know my body is made in the image and likeness of God, yet we call the locus of sin in ourselves "the flesh." We consume Jesus with our bodies, and just as often, it seems, we deny him with them. What remains in the balance between seeing my body as a battleground and seeing it as a blessing is a confusion and a longing—a confusion about how to embrace both these truths of my experience inside my body and a longing to know myself fully, body and soul, in the healthy perspective that it seems should be natural for someone who considers herself a beloved daughter of the Father.

For the longest time, I thought I was alone in that confusion and longing, that it was wholly based on my individual experiences and odd responses to them. But recently, I've witnessed the conversation about women and their bodies and how it affects their spiritual lives surface over and over again in the world around me. A whole lot of women seem to share my experiences and confusion and have decided that it is high time we stop keeping it all a secret and start doing some honest truth-telling about the experience of life as a Christian inside a female body.

Most of the honest storytelling I found, however, was some version of the spiritual relativism of "so your body is good, and it knows what will make you happy and whole, and being whole is what holiness really is, so go ahead and follow its lead, wherever that takes you."

While there is truth in the assertion that our bodies are inherently good in nature, there is equal truth in the reality that they are also fallen in nature; we still possess a tendency to allow ourselves to be ruled by our desires and thus fall into sin. Catholic thinking is distinct in its understanding of and teaching on what it means to pursue holiness and life in Christ inside our human flesh. The Catholic perspective on the human body is meant to allow us to chart the course of life in the tension between these two realities in a way that leads to a deeper intimacy with God and an ever-growing life of grace that we hope will lead us to eternal communion with him.

I found that many Catholic women feel much as I have— alone and secretive in their questions and confusion about their bodies and their experiences of faith inside them, and unable to grasp tightly enough to the side of the spectrum that sees their bodies as a blessing rather than a battleground. They are hungry to hear the truth and to tell their stories. While there is ample Catholic literature that explains the theological perspective on the body, there are few stories of the journey of a woman to spiritual and bodily wellness that fully embrace this view.

This book is my story, which I have been processing over the last year as I took a journey back to myself, back from burnout and shame and secret-keeping about my experiences to hope and healing and health. It is not a journey whose destination has been reached, whose lessons have all been learned and checked in neat red rows. I am less a seasoned sage at the end of her journey and more like a circus acrobat standing in the middle of a tight rope stretched taut between two points, learning to keep my footing as I maneuver back and forth, between a deepening understanding of the integration of body and spirit and the opposite pole of, well, basically coming undone. My legs are getting stronger, though, and I am beginning to learn to balance. I am getting better at journeying into myself body and soul, of undoing and unraveling myself to reveal a new layer that needs to be stripped away.

The most surprising thing I have learned is there is no spiritual wellness without the wholeness of a fully integrated body and soul. We cannot pursue spiritual wholeheartedness and intimacy with God living in bodies that bear shame, bodies we have come to see as enemies to our wellness. We were created as body and soul at once, and both aspects of our humanity are marked with the fingerprints of God.

Today, women are surrounded by a world that at both ends of a spectrum markets to us a complete disconnection of our physical and spiritual realities. On one end, the world of religion and faith mark the flesh as the enemy of our goodness, the weakness of our beings that most often keeps us from God. One the other end, the secular world tells us that the body is simply a pretty package from which we are meant to derive the most pleasure possible, and therefore, we can mold, manipulate, posture and maneuver it in whatever way we please to get the temporary pleasure we most desire right now.

What these two extremes have left us with is a world full of vaguely unsatisfied Christian women who feel out of sync and uncomfortable inside their physical bodies and yet can't put their finger on the heart of the disconnection. We can all readily admit that the notion of standing naked and exposed, both in our physical bodies and as our true selves, is a daunting proposition fraught with wounds and emotional weight we cannot quite seem to overcome. Many of us find ourselves frustrated that as grown women, the smallest emotional trigger can turn us back to insecure little girls who flush with shame. Food and weight, clothing and body shape, sex and intimacy, friendship and comparison—our lives are ripe with experiences that both bless and curse us at once, and leave us feeling like strangers who occupy a body that is mostly foreign to us and oddly out of our control.

If this is you, you are not alone. There is a whole host of women feeling it with you, and we are ready to tell our stories and look for the way back to the integrity of body and soul that is our heavenly inheritance.

Various women have graciously offered to share their stories throughout this book precisely so you can see that this journey back to our physical selves is a universal undertaking, one that every honest woman must come face-to-face with at some point in her life. These are women who are married and single, biological mothers and adoptive mothers, younger and older, living diverse experiences. And yet each of us has had our moments of reckoning, and are still having them, with the incarnational reality of our female bodies and what life looks like inside them. We have all battled wounds of shame, won some ground, and found the places where we still have work to do.

St. Teresa Benedicta of the Cross, who was, before religious life, Edith Stein, said in her 1932 essay, *Spirituality of the Christian Woman*, regarding the significance of woman, "We cannot evade the question as to what we are and what we should be." Yet we often feel quite pressured as women to evade those deep questions and just get about the business of living. And we ourselves sometimes prefer to evade them, because peeling away our masks and coping skills and digging deep for the truth is often a painful process, and one that, perhaps rightly, we feel there just isn't the time for.

But what if, in all truth, this was our only actual job here on earth? What if the work God has set out for us is to stop evading the questions of what we are and what we should be and to begin, as women, to prayerfully seek, if not answers, the nuggets of truth in the questions themselves. What if we gave ourselves the permission to ask hard and deep questions about these bodies we inhabit and what God intends for them, to have vastly different and yet eerily similar experiences inside them, and to never quite figure it all out? What if we rejected the demand that seems ever-present in the world around us to get ourselves together once and for all, shove our bodies inside a shiny gift box, no matter how ill-fitting, wrap them and make them pretty, and just be quiet already about the struggles and the pain and the confusion we feel?

If my conversations with women are any indicator, we are ready to listen to St. Teresa's counsel and seek out the truth of what we are as women and what that means we should be in the pursuit of holiness and wholeness. In this book we are already asking the questions, and fingering the veil of the mystery of God for the answers. As we do, we are walking back to the Garden of Eden together and trying to remember who we were when we were Eve, living naked and unashamed in the female form before God and man.

Together, we will ponder what we are and what we should be.

~ A NOTE BEFORE YOU BEGIN ~

Each chapter begins with a consideration, a question about our experience of faith and our bodies as women, and the thoughts that accompany that question. We begin to dig deeper into that consideration with an imaginative look at Scripture and what it might reveal to us about the meaning and the mystery behind the question we are considering.

From there, we take what we have found and look at how it might apply to us as women who want to more fully experience intimacy and harmony in our spiritual and physical lives. At the end of each chapter you will find the story of one woman and what she has discovered on her own journey of faith and physicality. The women you will meet in this book are a diverse group, and I know you will be blessed by them.

Lastly, at the end of each chapter you will find a section labeled "Further Up and Further In" (after a quote from C.S. Lewis). These are Scripture readings, journaling, and reflection questions to take to your personal prayer time. They are also perfect for gathering and studying the book together with a small group of women.

Every aspect of the book is meant to draw you deeper into the mystery of what it means to be woman, body and soul, and open your eyes to the great gift of that God-designed mystery and masterpiece. This is my desire for you because it is the desire of the God who created you and delights in you. Let us begin.

CHAPTER ONE

NAKED AND UNASHAMED

Women and the Eden Instinct

So God created humankind in his image,
 in the image of God he created them;
 male and female he created them.

—GENESIS 1:27

But for the man there was not found a helper as his partner. So the Lord God caused a deep sleep to fall upon the man, and he slept; then he took one of his ribs and closed up its place with flesh. And the rib that the Lord God had taken from the man he made into a woman and brought her to the man.

—GENESIS 2:20–22

And the man and his wife were both naked, and were not ashamed.

—GENESIS 2:25

· · · · ·

When I was a small child, we lived just down the street from my grandmother. We went often to her house to play in her yard and savor the crispy goodness of the sugar cookies she kept in the freezer just inside the back door. But the spot we longed for most, the spot that belonged to us and was where we belonged, was under the branches of the grand pecan tree whose shade filled her backyard.

My grandmother died when I was a little more than three years old, and her house was sold a few years later. We moved not long after that. I do not have many clear memories under that pecan tree—a fourth birthday party where a man parked a miniscule carousel on a trailer in its shade, all the times I wed the neighbor boy standing tiptoe on the tree roots holding a bouquet of wilting weeds while his sister and my cousins officiated. I don't know if it is my personal memory of that pecan tree that drapes it in safety and goodness in my mind or the collective family memory surrounding it that has dressed up my own foggy ones more beautifully than they deserve. But I know this: the smell of warm dirt and the prick of grass on the back of my thighs can bring me right back to the feeling of safety and joy—real, borrowed, or imagined—that I knew when I was tucked under the reaching arms of that tree.

Because of this memory, it makes sense to me that God would have designed, before he breathed humanity into existence, a garden of goodness to be their dwelling place. Just as I look back with foggy but curious wonder at that pecan tree in my grandmother's backyard, so I consider the Garden of Eden and its inhabitants.

It is that fog, that uncertainty about who we were in the garden, and the question of who Eve was that has been haunting me for some time now. I try to figure what I know of her in the same way I try to divine the truth of the unfamiliar familiarity I have with that pecan tree. How much of what I know of Eve is completely imagined, assumed, or created from blind feelings? Sure, I have the book of Genesis to guide me. It gives me a healthy glimpse at the first woman and a bit of her life in Eden. But even then, what of my interpretation is borrowed from a collective Christian understanding of who she was? What, if anything, do I know of Eve that is real and unique to me? Is there some instinct from the heart of the first woman that is imprinted on my spiritual and physical DNA? And if it turns out that most of what I know is simply a longing to know more of her, a female fancy to understand this "Mother of All the Living" who was all of us women at once at creation, is there something real in that?

I am certain I possess a kind of Eden instinct that draws me back to her, with a desire to understand what it means for me to be woman after her. I have come to think that all of us women might be imbued with an innate sense that if we could somehow clear the fog of the Eden memories and untangle Eve from them in order to know her better, we might find that we know ourselves better too. We have Mary as mother and guide-post of womanhood, and yet still, for me, there is a longing for the first woman, to know what it was like to be women when God's fingerprints were still fresh on our skin and we lived our Eden existence, when our flesh was free from the concupiscence of sin and the entire world lived in its original innocence. I am curious to know woman as she was when God dreamed her into existence.

If we are to follow that curiosity, to begin such an unraveling, we must begin in Genesis, at that moment in which man and woman came to be. Let us consider, then, Eve at creation.

~ CONSIDERING CREATION ~

In the Genesis account, Eve is God's final and most eagerly anticipated creation. The story of creation commences with the

Spirit of God moving across the void. We tend to think of this as the beginning of God in our Christian knowledge of him, yet because we recognize that God exists outside of time and space, and that God is immutable and unchangeable, we know that this cannot be the true beginning of God, who always was, always is, and always will be. What we know of the God who has always existed is that he is good, he is love, and he always has been.

When we consider creation from that perspective, it takes on a new significance. Everything that God created was born of his love and born from his goodness. And every created thing is born into goodness for the purpose of love. The whole created world was pleasing to God in that respect, so much so that "it is good" becomes the refrain of the creation story.

God moves across a void and delineates spaces in wide swaths—sky, sea, land. In increasing detail, creativity, and wonder, he begins to fill the world with his goodness. Plants and trees and the flowers that bloom on them. Stars and constellations, wind and waves, and the creatures that fill the sea. Daisies and dandelions, Venus flytraps and crimson roses. Tadpoles that turn into toads and starfish and dolphins and anemones that swish their colors with the currents. Then he fills the sky with birds who build nests and lay eggs in those trees—magpies and toucans and bald eagles and tiny, flitting hummingbirds. Bees begin to buzz, and beetles shine on forest floors. Then he waves his hand over the earth, and giraffes roam the savanna on one side while buffalo herds trample the plains on the other. Polar bears romp through the ice at its tip, and penguins splash into the water on the reverse pole.

And then, in what I imagine is clearly meant to be a crescendo of the symphony of creation—in which both action and senti-ment reach unparalleled levels that draw us up and out of ourselves to be lost in the glorious rush of it all—"male and female he creates them, in his image he creates [us]."

While God does not repeat the refrain "it is good" when it comes to the creation of man, it is, of course, a presupposed fact, because he states that they have been created in the image of God, who we know has always existed as goodness and love. It is interesting to consider that God created them "in his image" and "male and female" in Chapter 1 of Genesis, while the story of the creation of man and woman as distinct and separate forms does not appear until chapter 2 of Genesis.

This double-sided perspective suggests the timeless reality of God. From outside of time, humanity in its male and female forms, both created in his image, were thought of and planned for. Woman does not come along after man in the way a post-script tags on to the important part of a letter, or the encore is a short redo at the end of a stellar performance. No, from eternity man and woman were thought of by God, and at a given point in time, his creative impulse brought them into being along with, yet different from, the rest of the created world.

God brings man into being in a culmination of his creative force, and an increasing desire for relationship with his crea-tures. Everything else in creation simply springs forth from his word, coming to be as soon as he speaks it into being. Man, however, is fashioned. God considers man as he forms him. He molds the dirt of the earth into a human form with his hands, covers it with his touch, imprinting his image on it as he does. Then he breathes life into man. Here is our evidence that man is unique in all of creation. He is brought to life by the breath of God. God fills man with his own life, exhaling himself into humanity, in order that man might live.

What a distinct difference from the way the rest of creation comes to be! Men are fashioned and filled with the life of God and then given dominion over the rest of creation. God offers man to creation as its caretaker and creation to man as his source of well-being. And he delights in the fact that man bears his image.

And yet—oh, what an "and yet" it is! After all that progression from void to more detailed and imaginative creation, to breathing his life into a human and fashioning him in his likeness, God turns and looks at the created world, and for the only time in the whole creation narrative, his response is that it is not good. "It is not good that man should be alone," he declares in Genesis 2:18, and he sets about fashioning him a helper.

Stop for a moment and think what this might mean. God looked at the world he had created, teeming with life, stars flung across the heavens, every bird and bug and animal and flower in its most glorious state, the rivers and mountains and valleys and seas, and man—perfect in his reflection of the image of God— he looked at all of that, and saw that it was incomplete, that something was still missing. Before the Lord of the universe could sit back and rest, knowing his creative work was done, he longed for one more thing—he longed to bring woman to life.

At the culmination of God's creative love, we arrive at the shaping of woman, whom God forms from the rib bone of man to be helper and partner to him when no other created being suffices to fill that void. In all the world, nothing exists that can fulfill the need for woman. So God again sets about fashioning a being, this time, putting man into a deep sleep, opening him up, taking from him a rib bone, and shaping it into woman.

It is interesting that woman is not molded, but pieced together, starting from the strength of bone, the life-giving core of marrow, and becoming, layer by layer, softer and fuller, more and more of the image of God as he brings her to life. She is formed from the rib, the bone meant to protect the lungs of man into which God first breathed his own life. Woman is gifted to man and all of creation as helper, protector of the life of God within it, made to expand to cradle growth and contract to blow away what is not life-giving, strong but pliable enough to withstand the pressure of the responsibility with which she is charged.

And when God sees woman, what he sees is not simply spirit, but her physical body, itself a reflection of him. Rather than proclaiming its goodness himself, he leaves the refrain to Adam, who stands in place of all humanity as he proclaims with joy her name, "Woman," spoken for the first time in gratitude for the gift that she is. For woman is the only aspect in all of creation, its final, sweet note, that God gives to the rest of the created world as gift. "Here," he says, "I see you are missing something. Here she is. My woman. Now you are all I ever imagined you would be."

In the physical existence of woman, God's longing for a relationship with the created world and his desire for the good of humanity are met, and he is able to rest. Woman becomes gift not just to the world, but also to God himself, who finds his last longing fulfilled and rests in his satisfaction.

~ A Walk in the Garden ~

The created world complete, there is nothing left but the living for man and woman. Wonder for a moment about that first morning Eve woke up and was woman. Did she instinctively know who she was? Did she understand fully what it meant, this name of hers, "Mother of All the Living"? Did she run her fingers through her hair and twirl it up off her shoulders in a knot, as women do? Did she know straight away what her feet were and that the curve of her neck was lovely in its softness and that her hips could delight her with their sway? Did she know what her breasts were for, that they had the capacity to nourish new life?

What in all of creation did woman run to first? Did she smell a rose and only after learn it had thorns? Did she pet a soft kitten and giggle when it licked her hand or stand in silent awe at the running rivers as she learned the sound of their song? What did she eat first, and what did it taste like, that first perfect bite of the first perfect food? Was it a sticky, sweet orange, and did she let it drip down her chin and onto her neck without hesitation while she sucked its goodness from the pulpy flesh? Or did she pull a crunchy carrot up by its green top, wash it in the river and break it between her teeth, delighted by its decisive snap and crispness?

When Eve stood before Adam for the first time and let him look full upon her, did she know without a doubt how her mind and heart and body should respond to him? Was total self-donation easy and natural and without reserve for this first woman? Did she understand the intimacy of love and the pleasure of sex from the get-go? Did she know how to give with her body and receive with her body while her mind and her heart stayed right there in the moment too? What did woman's first sexual climax feel like?

And what did it look like for God to be fully present to woman in the garden? Did Eve hear his voice, or did she not need to because she lived in perfect communion with him? Did she understand his love for her fully, and how did she respond to it? Did he teach her about creation and what it means to be human as she walked with him alone in the garden? Did she understand the Trinity? What did Eve look like when she prayed?

While I cannot know the answers to all of these questions, here's what I think we can know: Eve in Eden is woman in her perfection. God, even before he made humanity, creates a garden where they will live. He fills it with all the good things they will need. Eden is creation at its perfection, and Eve is woman in her unblemished form. The last note of the creation song states that the man and his wife were both naked and they were not ashamed. Nakedness without shame. This is how woman was meant to live. This is the perfected state of our humanity—vulnerable, open, aware of our bodies and ourselves and understanding of others. Intimately free to be who we are before God. So, yes, I think Eve probably knew and understood right away who she was and what it meant to be woman, physically and spiritually. I think she knew the beauty of creation and enjoyed it freely and fully. I think she knew exactly how to love Adam, and, yes, I think they had fantastically pleasurable sex.

Consider Eve. While she lives under obedience to God's single command to her, she lives in perfect communion with her Creator. The garden itself is the best of the created world, and Eve lives in perfect harmony with creation. The creature in perfect assent to the will of the Creator enjoys the fruits of his creation without blemish. Eve enjoys that same harmony with Adam. He too is a creature living in his ideal state with the Creator and his creation. Their unitive bond is unbroken, and it mirrors perfectly the consummate love of God for them. In this state of communion with her Creator, his creation, and her fellow creature, Eve attains the last blessed gift of Eden—living in perfect harmony with herself—naked and unashamed.

This, I think, is every woman's great longing, our Eden instinct. Before woman became women who mirror God in a million glistening ways like snowflakes strung across time, there was a single woman, and womanhood meant this singular thing— the female soul joined to the female body in a perfect communion of being that made her capable of intimacy, communion, harmony, and self-awareness without the pain of shame. She lived naked in both aspects of self—her soul bare before her God and her body bare before the world.

I believe each of us, now unique in our womanhood in as many ways as there are women, still possess one common quality—the longing for that harmony. We feel it deep within us, the instinct to live free of shame, naked and vulnerable before our God and the world. The longing to know ourselves fully and not be afraid of who and what we are is a calling inside every woman. It is the map back to Eden imprinted on our souls and desired by our flesh. We long to know what it meant to be woman when we were Eve—to have that relationship with God, with man, with ourselves, with food and love and sex and our bodies. Eden's blessing calls us, and we spend our lives, if we are pursuing God earnestly, trying to unravel what it means to be Eve, to live naked and unashamed before him.

The task for us is that womanhood doesn't come to us the way it came to Eve. We are not born being woman as she was but instead are born into a becoming, a process that is constant and ongoing in our lives. And as we become, our minds learn, our hearts expand in their capacity to give and receive love, and our bodies undergo a near constant metamorphosis. Womanhood becomes a holy work of learning how to become ever more who we were when we were Eve. As much as we joke about women being a mystery to men, I think the truth is that we are just as often a mystery to ourselves, a beautiful, holy mystery whose revelation is at once sacred and confounding to us. Perhaps it might make us envy Eve, who simply *was* woman from the first moment of her incarnation. But this journey into who we are is such a worthy walk for us. And we are not without a map.

We all bear the same mark on our bodies and souls that made it possible for Eve to live in that harmonious communion of Eden. We, like her, bear the image of the Triune God. We are imprinted with divine life and infused with the capacity to love as the Father loves. And with that map in hand, we can follow our Eden instinct right into the heart of what it means to be a woman, the instinct that beckons us to who we were when we were Eve.

~ In His Image ~

One of my favorite details of the creation narrative is that God reveals himself as the Trinity at the moment he chooses to imprint his image on mankind. For the only time in the narrative, rather than referring to himself in the singular form, the Lord declares, "Let us make man in *our* image, according to *our* likeness." (Genesis 1:26; emphasis added).

There is something mysterious and profound, yet joyful and playful too, about considering God at work in a divine conversation between Father, Son, and Spirit, with creation as the spark of the love shared between the Trinity. Then to consider that after such a flurry of creative love, the Holy Trinity, three Divine

Persons, pauses to consider what he still longs for, what desire of his heart is unmet, and proclaims within himself, Father to Son to Spirit, "Let us create man in our image and likeness." He proceeds with a certainty and precision, to create humanity, in both its male and female forms, to be his image bearers on earth and live in relationship with him.

This movement of divine action back and forth among the three persons of the Trinity, the movement that brings humanity into being and stamps us with his image, is a flow of creational, incarnational, and relational life. In its flow, humanity is endowed with that same gift of divine life. We are all creational, incarnational, and relational beings. Humanity is the Trinity's love letter to itself, the concrete result of the creative love of God the Father sparking the incarnational love of God the Son, which releases the relational love of God the Spirit. That capacity is imprinted on the human soul and imbues each person uniquely with God's image.

"Male and female he created them" (Genesis 1:27). Distinct beings, created with equal parts divine, but mixed with a different recipe. That is man and woman, male and female. Both woven into creational, incarnational, and relational beings, but reflecting and projecting their divine image differently into the world. Woman is a being unique in her capacity to mirror these three aspects of God into the world and back to him in a way that delights and pleases both him and the rest of humanity. And these qualities are the road map to following our Eden instinct back to the fullness of our womanhood.

When I became pregnant, I thought for sure that motherhood would teach me what it meant to be a woman. As my body rounded out into its life-giving shape and a tiny human began to squirm inside me, I felt full with the reality of what it meant to be woman. I believed fully in my innate strength and the ancient wisdom of womanhood to guide me through pregnancy in the ritual of natural birth that I was certain would empower me not just as a mother, but as a woman. I was twenty-three and not sure what exactly I was expecting from that transformation, but I wanted to believe that pregnancy and birth would enlighten me if only I surrendered to the process fully and trusted my body to do what it was made to do.

By the time my first son was born, I had spent countless hours strapped to monitoring equipment and ultrasound machines. My blood pressure had skyrocketed, and there was an army of medical experts hovering over me trying to keep me healthy for the sake of the life growing inside me. Instead of the strength of sweat and blood and the warrior's cry, I gave birth in a rush of calls and bleeps, with my arms strapped down and the lower half of my body numb. My baby was whisked away to the bright lights and warm incubators of neonatal intensive care as I shook with the aftereffects of anesthesia, and a doctor pushed her fist into the incision across my pubic bone that had mysteriously decided to rip open.

I was a mother, but I had never felt more like a child in my life. I was scared, in need of being cared for, the object of everyone's concern. I could accept that this intervention had been medically necessary in my head, but in my heart, I was bitterly disappointed that my body had been incapable of the strength of woman and the way of the warrior I had dreamed childbirth would be. My body and my spirit had been unable to bring themselves into agreement, and the shame shrouded my transition to motherhood with the sense that as a woman, I had failed.

When I brought that baby boy home, only eleven months into being a wife and now a new mother too, that feeling of failing to become a real woman trailed me into our home. It showed up in the laundry being tumbled in the dryer for the third time instead of neatly folded in the drawers. It hovered nearby when breast-feeding was a challenge and my baby screamed relentlessly through the night. It clung to me with the pounds of weight that didn't shed quickly in the postpartum months like people promised they would.

I felt betrayed by womanhood, as though it pretended to be for all women but only settled on a few select favorites. I had not been picked for the team, just like the little girl standing on the line alone waiting to be chosen for kickball. The one experience I was sure would be my rite of passage into some mysterious world of strength and beauty and poise I had not yet learned to own for myself and my body had been anything but that. And "Mother of All the Living" felt far from who I was.

But with time and grace and not a few tears, a dawning came over me. It was not the physical act of becoming a mother or the way in which I gave birth that made me a woman, although experiencing those things in a more positive way certainly could have facilitated that process. But my becoming, my growing understanding of womanhood, was based in the imprint of the life-giving God on my incarnate body and its capacity to create, relate, and live in harmony. My sense that I had not made the cut was based not in my body's inability to fit a baby's head into my pelvic bones and facilitate its birth, but in the shame that blinded me to the fact that every day I was using that body to continue to create life for my little family, and to offer relational love to my husband and child. I didn't see myself as what a woman should be because I could not see the way my female heart and body were living in Eden harmony right there in my own little home, with my people, in the way only I could. Because my idea of what my body should have done to birth my little boy into this world was profoundly different than that reality, I fell into a perception of myself that disconnected me from God's truth about who I was as a woman.

Womanhood comes to us in our longing to create, to give and nurture life. For many women, the apex of that desire is the actual birth of a child, in which our bodies so completely mirror the salvific love of God for humanity as we grow pregnant with hope and then in blood and pain bring life to the world. But the longing lingers much deeper in us, and even outside of childbirth, we find our womanhood in creation, and quite often find ourselves most intimately connected with God when we are birthing something new into the world. And we birth life in so many ways that have nothing whatsoever to do with whether and how our bodies physically give birth to a child.

Becoming woman, it seems, has much more to do with our capacity to be creative in the way we love more than anything else. We are constantly called to give and nurture life in our respective spheres, and it often demands that we forget ourselves in the process. Yet forgetting ourselves is the very thing that can leave us feeling "less than" a woman. Our ability to engage in creational love is unique in that, as women, we offer our bodies and hearts to give others life while still expressing fully who we are in the unique ways that are ours alone. Those who are teachers, teach with a creative love and enthusiasm that is uniquely ours. Those who are writers, write with eyes that see the world only as we see it and wrap words creatively around that vision. Mothers share maternal love with a distinct flavor that belongs to only us. Professors, lawyers, entrepreneurs, farmers, artisans and any other thing that a woman becomes in life and brings her creative force to are each a unique reflection of God in our world in the form of female flesh.

Whatever it is we do on this earth is born of who we are, and we are all a uniquely creative reflection of the curious love of God the Father. When we remember that we live in his image by mirroring that creative love back to him in the way only we can, we find ourselves embracing womanhood without shame.

~ SARAH'S STORY ~

I've been at war with my body for as long as I can remember. I went off to kindergarten with a smile on my face and thighs that, even then, rubbed together when I walked. By the end of elementary school, I was fat, with wild, curly hair, glasses, and a painful awareness that my body was bad and wrong—decidedly not like the other girls' bodies. Through the onset of puberty and the realization that my hormones were hopelessly out of whack, to infertility and pregnancy loss, the inability to breast-feed when I finally had a child, and a diagnosis of diabetes in my midtwenties, my body has always let me down.

And bodies, I grew up learning, could not be trusted. Not the body of my mother, which ultimately betrayed us both when she was only thirty-two years old—leaving me an orphan. Nor that of my father—the weakness and frailty of his flesh leading him time after time to the drugs that dulled his pain and destroyed his life. I learned that bodies would only lead to heartache in the end.

By the time I finally became pregnant with the first child born into our arms, my body, far from being a temple for God's Spirit to dwell, was a frustrating source of disappointment and shame, a constant reminder of all I lacked.

Scripture is woven throughout with imagery reinforcing the sacredness of our bodies beginning with the beginning. "And it was very good." Surely, this could not mean me, in all my embarrassing largeness and fleshiness and realness. Surely these bodies that betray us could not be the apex of what God—who imagined the galaxies, and filled the oceans, and is the very force holding the universe together—called good. What is goodness if it applies to this flesh I drag through life, an albatross around my neck?

But my daughters are helping me find Eve and understand that goodness: my firstborn and then her sister, in all their newness and femaleness, coming as they have into this world, naked and unashamed. I see the joy they take in their bodies, discovering the ways they can touch and be touched by the created world. My daughters love their strong legs and full eyebrows, and they smile with joy at the sight of themselves. The innocence and love in their eyes, their unspoken awareness of being "very good" has broken my wall down. Finding Eve's goodness in them has caused me to look inward, to search for some remnant of Eve inside of me too.

To my absolute shock, I am finding her: when I fill a pitcher with fresh flowers and inhale their pure smell, like she did in the garden—moments when my mind, soul, and body are in harmony and I know that all are present and all are loved. I first found Eve in my daughters and now have found her in myself, in those moments when I treat my body like someone I love and someone who loves me back.

~ FURTHER UP AND FURTHER IN ~

Read chapters 1 and 2 of Genesis slowly. What elements of the creation story stand out for you? What are you seeing for the first time? What are you seeing in a new way?

Have you ever wondered about Eve and who she was? Which questions asked in the chapter caught your attention? What would you ask about her that wasn't asked here?

What does it mean to you that you are created in the image and likeness of the Triune God? How do you think that your distinctly feminine identity affects that? How is your female body a reflection of that truth?

How do you reflect the creational and relational love of the Trinity in your life? In what ways is your physical body involved in your expression of that love?

CHAPTER TWO

CONSUMING THE LIE

Shame and the Disintegration of Womanhood

So when the woman saw that the tree was good for food, and that it was a delight to the eyes, and that the tree was to be desired to make one wise, she took of its fruit and ate; and she also gave some to her husband, who was with her, and he ate.

—GENESIS 3:6

Then the eyes of both were opened, and they knew that they were naked; and they sewed fig leaves together and made loincloths for themselves.

—GENESIS 3:7

To the woman he said,
"I will greatly increase your pangs in childbearing; in pain you shall bring forth children,
yet your desire shall be for your husband, and he shall rule over you."

—GENESIS 3:16

· · · · ·

I don't remember exactly how old I was when I almost drowned. It was barely spring in the South but, in typical fashion, prematurely warm enough for a family picnic at a campground and a dip in the pool. We piled into our car, trailed by family friends, and drove the hour away to pine woods, outdoor grills, and the biggest swimming pool I had ever seen. I awaited that swimming pool with such girlish excitement that the moment our car came to a stop in the parking lot, I bolted toward it without looking back to the moms unloading armfuls of gear from the car. Without a moment's hesitation, I jumped straight into that wide blue coolness—and promptly sank.

I don't know how long it took me to realize my feet were not going to reach the bottom to propel my head back above the water where I could breathe. Or to feel panic grip my throat as I remembered what a notoriously poor swimmer I was. What I do remember clearly was the moment the water did its saving work and held the weight of me up just long enough for my sputtering and gasping and flailing to be noticed by the other mom who accompanied us on the trip.

I was afloat long enough to see her drop everything she was carrying and rush toward the pool, and as I sank again, I knew she was coming in to rescue me. And instead of feeling relieved, for the first time that I can remember in my life, I burned with the shame of needing to be rescued.

This is just it, isn't it? How sin and disobedience do us in. We rebel against our dependency on God and decide to strike off on our own and try it our way, then find ourselves drowning and needing to be rescued. Dependent once again on our Creator and Maker—this time on his mercy to reach us where we have fallen and bring us back into the air of his life-giving love where we can breathe. Every time we disobey God and sin, we find ourselves right back in the place we tried to leave, utter dependency on him to maintain and keep us in communion with him—to keep us spiritually alive.

It bothered me much of my life that it was Eve who took the apple first. It seemed an unfair burden to put on women for the rest of the history of time that sin came into the world through us. But the truth is that Adam and Eve were equally culpable for their disobedience to God in the garden, and henceforth, men and women have lived in equally concupiscent forms, with bodies and souls whose passions must be wrangled by the will in order to fully assent in obedience to God.

But it is also true that Satan played a role in the first sin and that he still does today. His wiliness and cunning were the lures that Eve and then Adam followed into disobedience to God. Eve was not the temptation that caused Adam to sin, as we sometimes errantly believe; Satan was. What we see in the story of the fall is that Satan knows our capacity to sin lies in our ability to choose freely our desires and doubts over our love for God. And the desires and doubts we are most likely to give into are unique for men and women. Eve was wooed into sin by the lie that what she had and who she was as God had made her was not enough, and by her desire to have and be more. It was Satan's promise that the apple would make her more that thrust Eve into a spiral of desire that clouded her Eden instinct and left her prey to sin. Adam, on the other hand, in responding to Eve's offer of the apple, is not wooed into sin by *her*, but by his own greatest doubt and desire, which is whether it is enough to be dominant in all of creation and still dependent on God, or whether his desire for total domination without dependence is the real victory. In taking the apple from Eve, Adam allows his Eden instinct to be clouded by his desire to objectify creation and his fellow human so that he alone can rule over them.

With the fall, we are left with the question of what it now means to be human. And in our female bodies, we women are left to wonder what womanhood now means. What is the reality of life outside of Eden for us? What does it mean to pursue holiness inside flesh marked with both the image of God and the possibility of sin? And how is our Eden instinct marred by the war between our passions and our will?

Perhaps we'd rather not look so closely at the fall, recognize ourselves in the ugly reality of disobedience, but if we are to take a journey toward fully understanding our human and bodily selves, a close look is indeed in order, bravely and honestly facing who we become when we sin.

~ CONSIDERING THE FALL ~

What we know definitively of life in Eden after creation was that Adam and Eve lived naked and without shame—in the full freedom of their original innocence; that they enjoyed their humanity in its perfect state, living in communion with God, his creation, and one another as result. This was God's plan for Adam and Eve, to enjoy an eternity in which they freely responded to the love he gave them, living in an intimate relationship. Giving and receiving in complete self-donation, humanity becoming a mirror of the Trinitarian relationship, and Adam and Eve shared a nuptial intimacy that reflected in physical form the communion of love that humanity enjoyed with God.

It was precisely the freedom to give and receive love within their physical bodies, in the most tangible sense of the word, that made Adam and Eve images of God in the world. Before their existence, the word held no visible image that could lift the imagination to the divine mystery of a God who loves freely. John Paul II said of the human bodies of Adam and Eve that they alone are "capable of making visible what is invisible: the spiritual and the divine."[2]

And because the key aspect of God's relationship with humanity is that he gave his love to us in creating us in his image and likeness, it is necessary that humans return God's love and embrace intimacy with him in complete freedom as well. Man must have free will to choose to love God and assent in obedience to God in order to be a physical sign of the divine reality of God's love.

Certainly there have been times when I was weighed down by the choice between the burden of my own sin or the choice to assent to God's will. When it seems so difficult to be born of love and mercy, I wish away my free will. Sometimes it would be so much easier to have no choice but to do what God asks of us. But the truth is, our faculty to choose the good and make it tangibly present here on earth is what endows our humanity with godliness. Love, dependency, and trust, and the intimate communion that results from them, are ours to have if we choose them freely. They cannot be thrust upon us against our will because then they are none of those things—they become instinctive and reflexive reaction rather than conscious relationship. Our ability to choose to love God in return for the way he has loved us is the heart of human existence. And it is only in our physical bodies that our souls come to supersede our desires and passions for other things and choose God first, that we exist fully as the *imago dei,* "the image of God."

The ability to choose the opposite of that goodness and total intimacy with God is a necessary part of our human reality. Until the fall from grace in the garden, our eyes were veiled to the full consequences of that choice, but now we live in the world outside of Eden, where our unveiled consciences are subject to the insistence of our desires, and we are ever aware of the consequences of our disobedience.

In the loss of our original innocence, we lost the life of living naked and without shame. Our bodies must now pursue holiness rather than simply take pleasure in it. And we are forever on a journey to pull back the fig leaf of shame and come out of the bushes where we have hidden ourselves from God to stand before him with repentant hearts and wait for his mercy to rescue us.

Can you just imagine for one moment what it was like for Eve to realize what she had done after she bit into that apple? For her eyes to be opened to her sin and for her to feel the burn of shame on her cheeks for the first time? What heartbreak it must have been for her to know her own capacity to live outside the will of God and feel her Eden life slip away so quickly. Did she gag on the bitter taste of her own pain? Did her stomach lurch in anxiety when she turned her head away from that apple, the testament to her sin? Did her eyes flash with anger at the self-satisfied serpent who surely sat hissing his pleasure back at her as she welled with tears for the first time?

Oh, precious woman, how we weep with you, your sinful sisters who know this pain all too well. We know it, too, the inexplicable foolishness of wanting what we know we don't need and how our minds can cloud with desire until it becomes doubt about what God really said. I used to look at Eve with a certain bitterness, blaming her for my own depravity. But when I am honest about my temptations and how easily they convince me that I know better than God, I can only embrace Eve with compassion and suffer with her what it is to know the shame of disobedience. Every time the word flies out that I know should stay in, every time I say yes to the thing I know I should say no to, every time I find delight in the things God clearly told me are not for me, I know the urge of Eve to find the nearest place to hide myself from God, the scourge of shame making me unable to bear intimacy with him.

But there is hope for us. While shame was never God's intention for us and we will always feel it as pain, it is also a sign that we remember Eden, that we possess a special sort of Eden instinct. Because shame is the place where we know that sin has disconnected us from God and the life of grace we lived in the garden, and it is also filled with the longing to get back to that original innocence and intimacy, even as we hide ourselves from God.

Genesis 3 tells us that when Adam and Eve had eaten the apple "their eyes were opened" and they recognized their own nakedness. So many times in the Gospels, Jesus talks about living with our eyes open, or "with eyes to see" as a positive spiritual posture (Mark 8, Luke 10, John 9), but in this instance in Eden, it is the unveiling of our passions and the destruction of our original innocence that is referred as "seeing." Before that moment, Adam and Eve lived completely at home in themselves and their physical bodies, and in communion with God and his creation. The first sin opens their eyes to the pain of shame and frees the temptations of desire in their souls. Never again will we humans be able to trust our "flesh" the way they had in Eden.

And yet, when we look more closely at God's response to the first man and first woman after their sin, what we find is a God who, while he is compelled to justice, is also driven by compassion. The truth is, while shame may result from our sin, it is also the force that compels us to fight to be rescued, just as my young legs kept propelling me back up and out of that water instinctively until someone could come save me from myself. While *we* feel like sin should make us hide from God and turn our face away from him, *he* is there longing to pull us out of hiding and bring us back to him. Psalm 18 even tells us that it is precisely God's initial delight in us that drives him to deliver us when we are losing the battle with our enemy: "He brought me out into a broad place; he delivered me, because he delighted in me" (Psalm 18:19).

So even in the state we now find ourselves as women, wavering between the truth of being made in the image and likeness of our good God and the shame of living in a world of concupiscence, we can use both ends of the spectrum to tune into our Eden instinct. The first sin destroyed the four-part harmony of Eve's original innocence, but it did not destroy our longing for it, our hope of it, or our instinct to look for our way back to it.

~ HIDING OUT IN EDEN ~

Satan's first question to Eve is "Did God say..." (Genesis 3:1) and in some biblical translations, "Did God *really* say...?" The first line of the same verse calls him (the serpent) "the most cunning of all the creatures." So what exactly was it that he was conning Eve into? The reality is, whether it was a defense of God or a denial of God, all Satan really needed from Eve was a response. As soon as she turns her attention to him and tries to answer his question, she has engaged his deceitful nature, and he knows just where to go next.

So while Eve answers him straightforwardly with the simple truth of what God has told them, Satan begins to chip away at the truth and tease out the doubts and desires of Eve's heart that will eventually make her turn away from God and turn to sin.

What was Eve thinking and feeling that particular day in the garden that made her susceptible to entertaining the serpent? Had she been wandering alone all day and feeling the weight of her loneliness? Had she been tasting the other fruits of the garden while she looked upon that one forbidden tree and wondered how its sweetness was different from the others? Had she gone out to look for God and gotten bored or distracted or confused and so turned to the first company she found? Did she bristle at the hiss of the serpent's cunning voice first and then respond, or did she not even know to be on her guard against him? What was the turning point where Eve's free will drew her away from God rather than toward him? From where did the disordering of her passions first arise?

Satan's next words to Eve are an offer for her to either assent to the will of God or assert her own will into the garden for the first time. "You will not die; for God knows that when you eat of it your eyes will be opened, and you will be like God, knowing good and evil" (Genesis 3:4–5). And here is where Satan's cunning nature is revealed: Eve needs nothing outside herself to be like God. She is already like God, made in his image and likeness. And yet Satan convinces her, as he does the rest of us so many times, that she is not enough as she is. She is not enough for God, she is not enough like God, and there is more she could and should be.

How often do we find the world around us hissing the same insinuation in our ears? Constantly, it seems. I know I hear the hiss of that lie far too often in my own ears. I may not be certain what it was that made Eve particularly susceptible to Satan's voice that day in Eden, but I do know the things that leave me with the tinge of doubt that opens the door for him: the sink full of dirty dishes left overnight, the argumentative stance I took toward my husband, the harsh word spoken to a child unde-servedly, the resentment I feel at my duty to serve others, the distraction from prayer and my less-than-saintly spiritual life. None of these things in and of itself is a full threat to the life of grace I am called to lead, but they are all places where Satan can curl himself up in a corner of my mind and begin to say to me, "Did God really say...? You will not die...you will be like God." Those questions prick my heart, and the doubt that I am really enough like God as I am seeps out, and with it, the desire to be more than I should be, the desire that leads me to grab at my own will instead of assenting to God's.

While the rest of the scene of the fall continues to take place in the Garden of Eden, Eve's life outside of Eden begins just after she turns back to the Tree of Knowledge, and for the first time since God fashioned her into being, she looks at some-thing with the eyes of desire rather than the heart of inno-cence and obedience. Her Eden life doesn't end with her physi-cally walking out of the garden; it ends the moment her heart chooses to be delighted by something other than God: "So when the woman saw that the tree was good for food, and that it was a delight to the eyes, and that the tree was desired to make one wise..." (Genesis 3:6).

What was different when Eve turned to look at the tree in that moment? Was there a sweet smell on the air or a certain shine to the lowest-hanging apple that attracted her eyes and drew out her desire? Was she particularly hungry? Had she not fed herself well that day or walked alone with God in the garden in the morning? Did she linger in the moment of this transition? Did she feel the shift in her soul with anxiety and longing all at once? Did you ever stop to wonder about this, the moment the first woman saw the world for the first time outside of God's vision and fell headlong into the first sin?

Eve takes the apple and eats of it after going down this spiraling thought path: seeing the tree's goodness, desiring its goodness, and that desire becoming the desire to be wise, wiser even than God. She opens her heart to her passions slowly, the desire unfolding within her, until she arrives at the heart of all desire, the thing we all convince ourselves of when we sin, that the thing we want is actually very good, and we can know better than God.

Did Eve's hand shake as she reached out to pull that apple from the tree? Or did she grab it greedily, lustily, acting while she was still convinced she was right and had the courage to do so? And what did that first bite taste like? Was it bitterly disappointing, the apple mealy and soft and not very sweet at all? Or did it feel good and tantalizing for just a moment, like she had gotten exactly what she wanted? Did she give the apple to Adam because it was exciting and she was racing with rebellious energy for the first time, or because she already felt the sinking feeling of guilt in her heart and she was determined not to feel it alone?

What we can know for certain is that life outside of Eden, which begins at this point, is full of questions and confusion and anxiety that Eve had never experienced when she walked in the obedience of the garden life. The consequences come in a quick cascade for Adam and Eve: shame of their nakedness, hiding themselves, falseness in their conversation with God, tension in their relationship with one another, identifying Satan as their enemy, and then God's justice. Eve, the mother of all the living, will suddenly know the creative, life-giving force inside her only in pain. She will labor to give birth to new life, and the intimacy between man and woman will be tainted by desire, manipulation, and a struggle for dominance and power. Eve, who was made to create and birth life, and live in consummate intimacy, is now all of us, who live ever trying to find our way between the two warring worlds within us, the one in which our instincts to be givers of life are pure and freely embraced and the one in which our desire clouds them with selfishness and lust.

~ Our Disintegration ~

In that heartbreaking moment, when Eve first looks down at her own body and sees it as bad, the flesh becomes, for the first time in human history, the object of a woman's shame, something other than her apart from who she was made to be, something that risks her goodness rather than houses it. Something to be covered and hidden rather than enjoyed and given freely in the security of love and untainted intimacy.

Before God ever calls her out of her hiding and confronts her with her sin, Eve is living the consequences of it, the disintegration of her personhood. God fashioned Eve purposefully, laying layer upon layer of her fleshly body over the strength of bone, giving her life from his life, and making her mother of all the

living for the good of humanity. Body and soul, God fashioned
Eve in his image as a giver of life and mirror of his goodness,
meant to love intimately and burgeon with creative purpose that
would birth beauty into the world, filling it with "the feminine
genius" that St. John Paul II in *Mulierus Dignitatem* defined as
receptivity, generosity, sensitivity and motherhood.

The consequence of sin is literally Eve's coming undone as
a person. She becomes "the opposite" (*dis*) of "made whole"
or "rendered complete" (*integrate*), or of being, literally,
"untouched" by sin.[3] She is now touched by sin, and the wholeness she enjoyed in Eden begins to fall apart. The moment she
looked at that apple tree and saw it with the eyes of desire
rather than the eyes of obedience, she lost that perfect harmony
with God's creation in which she had lived until that point. And
when she turns and hands sin to Adam in the form of that apple
and he readily receives it from her and takes it into his own
body, the perfect harmony Eve enjoyed in her human relationship is also undone.

With the act of sin complete, Genesis tells us that Adam's
and Eve's eyes are opened, and they feel their nakedness for the
first time. They respond by making themselves loin cloths from
fig leaves. Shame disintegrates Eve by destroying her harmony
with herself, pulling apart the integration of her body and soul,
separating her physical and spiritual awareness, and putting the
three aspects of her spirit—her intellect, will, and passions—at
enmity with one another for the first time. The fig leaf is Eve's
first experience of shame at who she is. It marks her womanhood
in its most intimate and vulnerable place as untrustworthy, and
her complete vulnerability, the full revelation of who she really
is, as unacceptable.

It is that shame that sends Eve into hiding from the God who knows she is no longer as he made her—unashamed, freely dependent on him and receptive to that dependency. But when God goes out looking for Adam and Eve, we also get the first glimpse of hope in the otherwise hard to swallow story of the birth of sin. God surely already knew exactly what had happened and where Adam and Eve were, but he goes out looking for them, calling them back to him straightaway. He does not leave them hiding in their sin and shame for more than a moment before he is after them, reminding them of who he is and who they are in him, creatures meant to live in communion with their Creator.

The last, heartbreaking witness to Eve's disintegration comes in her response to the Lord's searching for her. Eve, made and designed to live in perfect communion with her God, responds to him with diversion and blame, "The serpent tricked me," a response that is shaded with falseness, an attempt to cover her own culpability. She poses and postures before God, and the true death caused by sin becomes at once apparent to us.

No, the apple did not bring physical death to Eve, just as the serpent said it wouldn't. But it was the end of her life of perfect harmony with her God and her creator, the death of Eve's integrity as a woman, a descent into a new form of personhood that forever marks woman. God's declaration to Eve of the permanent consequence of her sin is the confirmation of this death and disintegration: "I will greatly increase your pangs in childbearing; in pain you shall bring forth children, yet your desire shall be for your husband, and he shall rule over you" (Genesis 3:16). The four-part harmony of Eve's Eden existence is placed in discord with the four-part consequence of her now concupiscent self; instead of living in perfect harmony with God, his creation, herself, and others, she now lives with shame of herself, pain in the action of procreation, discord in her human relationships, and distance from God.

God created Eve to live in the fullness of her Eden instinct, which is a life of perfect assent to his will and the full intimacy of consummate love with him. Consummation is the joining of two things into their highest form. Woman's instinctive state is complete and total trust of God's will for her and receptive intimacy with him. Our human state now marked by original sin, we find ourselves as Eve did at the fall, asserting our own wills where we should be assenting to God's, and consuming something other than God where we should be offering ourselves to him in consummate love.

We all now live in danger of believing the lie that we are not enough like God as we are and that something other than God will give us what we need to feel full and free. But we also live ever compelled back to God by our Eden instincts, remembering who we once were when we lived naked and unashamed. So we are ever fighting to come out of hiding and stand before our God when he comes after us, looking for us even in our sin and shame.

For many long years after that near drowning incident, I lived terrified and filled with shame at the thought of needing to be rescued. It fueled a perfectionism and addiction to competence in my life that made vulnerability and intimacy with God and others ever-challenging. While my journey has moved me ever further into trust and surrender to God, those tendencies are still an ongoing battle in my life. In the last year, they have overrun me to the point that my body ached with the weight of it, and I reached a phase of complete physical and emotional burnout.

In that season of my life, God sent me a new friend and mentor who offered guidance and maternal love to my tired, drowning heart. For the first time in a very long time, I was completely honest with someone about how undone I was. I beat back the shame of needing to be rescued and the desire to hide from my incompetency, and I bared myself before her, naked and not a little terrified. What her response to my vulnerable state taught me about God was that the only option outside of letting ourselves be rescued is death, but shame won't kill us if we let mercy save us. As a matter of fact, shame is our reminder that Eden was real, and it can be our hope if we let it be, because it reveals that we long to live again in the perfect assent and consummate love for which we were created, and that something is wrong with life outside that love.

After articulating the consequences of sin to Adam and Eve, God's compassion and mercy immediately begin to flow out toward them. Scripture tells us that he "made garments of skin for the man and his wife, and clothed them" (Genesis 3:21). Knowing that Adam's and Eve's new nature makes nakedness no longer safe for them, neither physically nor spiritually, he clothes them in garments of protection. He takes the fig leaves of their shame, which will do them no physical or spiritual good in the world where they must now live, and covers them in modesty and mercy. While these garments do not replace what was lost at the fall, and it seems the human heart will ever long for the safety and vulnerability of full nakedness, God's mercy covers us while we await our salvation.

It is a reminder that we do not have to be afraid of our instinct to fight to be rescued, that we do not have to hide in shame when we have jumped in where we should not have and cannot sustain ourselves on our own. We can step out from hiding and stand before our Creator and trust that while we still bear the marks of our concupiscence and the consequences of our sin, his mercy runs to us and covers us. He will always come back to rescue us, because he is the God who delighted in us at the moment of creation, when he layered complexity upon complexity over a single bone and gave us our being and existence, and the God who delights in us still, even as we learn to walk outside of Eden.

~ SHARON'S STORY ~

When I sat outside of my pastor's office some fifteen years ago, I had come to him not for confession, but to argue with him about why the church was wrong in its teachings. I didn't know that the shame from my past was what was driving me to fight against what I knew inside my heart was right. One moment I wanted to prove my point, arguing in my head that the selective reduction of the quadruplets I conceived to twins was not a form of abortion; then in the next moment, I wanted to run and hide.

Since then I have learned to recognize shame and its effects on how I see myself. Shame and guilt are different. Guilt reminds us that we did something wrong. Shame tells us that something is wrong with us. The world and I have a use for guilt. It was guilt that led me to talk to that priest, to make that appointment, even though I denied that was the reason why.

Because of my shame, I didn't know that God's forgiveness was waiting for me behind that priest's office door. My plans and arguments were no match for God's loving embrace through the kind words of that priest. That day, instead of hiding from God and covering myself with fig leaves, I told the naked truth of who I am, of what I had done, and my belief that no one could really love me.

Not only had I separated myself through the sins in my life, I had pushed God away after the death of one of my twins from sudden infant death syndrome. I thought that the God I didn't believe in was punishing me. Sin can do that, twist your mind and drive you from the truth, from God, from love.

As I sat in the grief of the death of my son and the secret shame of the death of my unborn babies while tending to my newborn daughter, I continued to feed myself the lie that I could not be loved. The scars of the sin almost drove my marriage apart. The blessing of another child and the ongoing day-to-day work of parenting kept us together, but we lived a life outside of Eden.

The moment I walked into that priest's office, something changed in my heart, and through the pouring out of my soul as I made my confession, admitting the truth of myself to God, my shame was released and I experienced sanctifying grace. I was no longer lying to myself or to God. I conversed with him and exposed my own naked truth to him. And I instantly knew God's love for me! God forgave me. God knew me and loved me anyway. And my life changed forever.

Further Up and Further In

Read Genesis chapter 3 slowly. What elements of the story of the fall stand out for you? What are you seeing for the first time? What are you seeing in a new way?

Have you ever wondered about Eve that particular day in the garden? Which questions asked in the chapter caught your attention? What would you ask about her that wasn't asked here?

Does shame affect your relationship with God and others? Have you ever seen shame as a positive emotion? How you might turn your perception of shame into a reminder of who you were truly created to be?

Where do you see God's mercy covering and protecting you in your life? Where are you fighting against being rescued? How might you let go and trust in God's goodness and desire to rescue you?

⎯⎯⎯ ∞ ⎯⎯⎯

CHAPTER THREE

THE NEW EVES AND THE BODY OF CHRIST
Re-Membering Ourselves

"And now, your relative Elizabeth in her old age has also conceived a son; and this is the sixth month for her who was said to be barren. For nothing will be impossible with God." Then Mary said, "Here am I, the servant of the Lord; let it be with me according to your word."

—LUKE 1:36–38

And Elizabeth was filled with the Holy Spirit and exclaimed with a loud cry, "Blessed are you among women, and blessed is the fruit of your womb. And why has this happened to me, that the mother of my Lord comes to me?"

—LUKE 1:41–42

My soul magnifies the Lord, and my spirit rejoices in God my Savior, for he has looked with favor on the lowliness of his servant. Surely, from now on all generations will call me blessed; for the Mighty One has done great things for me, and holy is his name.

—LUKE 1:46–49

· · · · ·

I don't know if I was the most excited eight-year-old ever to make her first Communion, but I can tell you this, I was definitely more excited than the average one. For one thing, I really did love Jesus as much as a little girl's heart can wrap itself around that mystery. For another, the tendencies toward spiritual perfectionism and people pleasing were already burgeoning in my wide-eyed, expectant little spirit, and I wanted so much to receive my first Communion well—the right way, the way that was expected of me.

So on the day of our rehearsal, I listened intently to the instructions of Sr. Mary Ellen, who stood in the sanctuary of the monolithic church where the occasion would occur and showed us how we would walk in a single-file line to the side steps and wait there until the spot just at the top was free, and then we would move along. From there, to the X marked in tape exactly perpendicular to the priest and the child receiving the Blessed Sacrament. And from there, to the spot where we would receive Jesus for the first time.

Then she illustrated how we were to hold our hands, right palm over left, and *up high*, she emphasized, so the priest would not have to bend down to look for them. When my turn came, I was determined to follow those instructions exactly as she had given them, so I marched behind the other children in my line and stood patiently at the white marble steps, hands at my side, no fidgeting.

When the space opened, I stepped deliberately to the first spot on the altar, then the next, and finally, I approached the sister who was now playing priest, and with great concentration, I put my palms atop one another just as she had demonstrated and raised them high to show my great desire to receive the

Eucharist, and to receive it right. The good sister chuckled at my effort and said something about how I had taken her instructions very seriously, as she lowered my outstretched hands ever so slightly.

That weekend, I walked with less confidence through the paces of altar stops along the way to my First Communion, and I held up my hands with great doubt about whether I was doing it just right. And then the priest, without checking their position, without affirming or correcting me, simply placed the host in my hands and said gently, "The Body of Christ." And there he was. Jesus. Waiting to be received by me. And how I held my hands seemed to matter very little if at all in that moment.

There is a picture of me, ringlet curls wreathed in tiny white flowers, dressed in a perfectly white dress I adored, standing outside church next to my godfather, also a Catholic priest. I am radiant. There is no trace of that doubt left on my smiling face. My hands folded in front of me like a prayer seem to know just what they are doing.

Somewhere in my adult life, I adopted the practice of receiving communion primarily on my tongue. While many view it as more reverent, I just saw it as the less likely way for me to mess up the process. And yet every single time I stand in that line, I waver for just a moment over the doubt that I am not opening my mouth right, that I am once again doing it wrong when I am only trying to do it right.

And every single time, Jesus just shows up, somehow, right there on my tongue, to be received by me. No one ever adjusts my jaw or my lips, or even looks at me funny. Over and over again, grace just descends easily and freely for my taking. And I remember what it is like to be radiant in the joy of that reception.

This is grace. This is how we re-member who we are. We are the women who never knew Eden but instinctually long for it in our heart of hearts. We are the women who have never known what it is to live outside of concupiscent bodies, who unlike Mary, conceived without sin, are sinful way more often than we are saintly. But we look to her as our new Eve, woman as woman was meant to be, and embrace her as mother on our journey back to grace, back to the heart of the Father through the Body of Christ and his beloved Bride, the Church.

This is how we re-member ourselves when we live in fallen flesh in a fallen world—by surrendering ourselves to the God who becomes incarnate flesh inside the womb of a woman, earns our salvation through his suffering, death, and resurrection, and leaves behind the gift of a mother to guide us and a Church that becomes his body in action, animated by the Holy Spirit, and gives us a tangible, breathing, living entity in which we can re-member ourselves to grace and to the goodness of God.

~ CONSIDERING INCARNATION ~

Imagine with me for a moment that you had never heard of Christianity or the Bible or the Christian worldview of creation. If that were the case and I had presented you with the two stories we have just discussed, creation and the fall, would you have ever guessed that the way this mess was all redeemed and made right was that thousands of years later in a specific point in time in a specific place on earth in the womb of a very specific woman, the same God who had made man for himself would make himself a man for men? I think you would more likely react with the popular phrase "Didn't see that one coming." In fact, most of the faithful Jewish people who made up the descendants of Adam and Eve didn't see it coming, and were and still are looking for an entirely different solution to the problem of our humanity than a man named Jesus who was born of a virgin named Mary. It's quite likely that any one of us with an honest faith can also say that there are many days we look to God and still wonder at his choice. The incarnation is no small truth to accept, especially when it becomes the core of your understanding of yourself and your salvation.

And yet here we are. The world has waited thousands of years, since the dawn of creation, to know just what the answer might be to the problem of our sin. God has offered hints throughout history, tales and stories and rescues and relief that serve to remind us that even after Eden's gates were blocked by a flaming sword, he remained present to his people—the ones he had formed and fashioned and called his own and clothed with compassion even after they had turned away from him. Throughout the Old Testament, God warns and sends signs of destruction in his just anger, but just as often, he speaks of the day he will bring us back to our homeland, the day we will once again be his people and he our God.

When God created man and then woman as his final act of creation, he wrote himself a love letter. Humanity was the only aspect of creation God made exclusively for himself, and his only desire was for us to live in consummate love with him. When we betrayed that love with sin, the heart of our God was left with an unrelenting desire for the creature he had made like himself to once again be like him. God is the impulse for the Eden instinct that plagues our hearts. As he longs for us and all creation outside of us groans with that longing, we remember somewhere deep ourselves that we are created for perfect union with him, and we long for it.

But just as the beginning of the world according to our creation story was not the beginning of God, it is also true that the moment of the annunciation of the angel Gabriel to the woman Mary was not the beginning of his plan for our salvation. As soon as we negated God's first love letter to himself with our sin, he took up the pen of mercy and began to write a love letter to us. A love letter of incarnation, that as St. Athanasius says, "touched all parts of creation, and freed and undeceived them from every deceit."[4] For this reason, when God the Father deemed that for a particular moment in the history of the world, he would send the Son to take on human skin and become incarnate in the womb of a woman, he was in need of a new Eve. He could not rewrite the love letter between himself and creation and leave one of the main characters missing.

So for the New Adam, there was a new Eve. Not a new nearly Eve, a saintly kind of woman with a particularly strong Eden instinct who came awfully close to Eve's original innocence, but a truly new version of Eden's perfect woman. While all of humanity that followed forth from Adam and Eve felt, as we do, the tug of the Eden instinct at work in their hearts, none had the bodily quality of original innocence to match that instinct, until Mary.

Mary's Immaculate Conception is a long misunderstood and underappreciated doctrine of the Catholic Church. The usual explanations of Mary as a new Ark of the Covenant—a perfect vessel created to house the holy of holies, God's presence with man—are rich and precise in all their correctness. Yet, Mary was not simply made perfect from conception because God could not bear the idea of entering a female body sullied by sin. She was made in the original Eden innocence and perfection of femininity because as God wrote the love letter of redemption to humanity, he wrote it in reverse of the original story of creation.

God dreamed up a world and then found himself longing still for the something that would be enough like him to love him, so he first formed Adam from the clay of the earth and breathed life into him, and then, seeing the last missing link, took a piece of Adam, flesh and bone of the first man, and layered slowly over it the intricate design of woman, he does the reverse in the act of the incarnation.

He forms first a woman who will be like him as Eve was, who even before the overshadowing that impregnates her with the Son, lives in consummate love with the Holy Spirit as Eve did in Eden. And when the moment comes for him to incarnate himself in her womb in order to return to us the possibility of an Eden life in eternity, the God who layered woman complexity over beautiful human complexity and then placed her in the safety of a garden becomes man, cell layered over cell in the safety of her womb. Genesis tell us that in the center of Garden of Eden stood the Tree of Life and the rivers that ran through Eden nourished the fruit of that garden. And here is our God, mercifully coming to save our mortal bodies from being locked out of that garden forever, in the perfect womb of a perfect woman, a new Eve nourishing our salvation in a New Eden.

In birth culture, it is common to call a woman's placenta "the tree of life." It is an organ created by a woman's body specifically to nourish the life she is gestating. Its thick strong connection to the umbilical cord mimics a trunk, and then the blood vessels fan out on the surface of the placenta itself, creating an image that evokes the branches of a tree, with the round organ creating the tree's foliage. That tree feeds the life growing in the garden of the woman's womb, surrounded by the waters of safety inside her amniotic sac. When the baby is born, along with the gorgeous human life, the nourishing blood of the placenta and the life-giving waters of the amniotic fluid must also flow out to complete the process.

The detail of the reversal of our creation process with the incarnation process cannot be ignored. Mary, the new Eve, gestates God in the garden of her womb, nourishing him with her own placenta, the tree of life her perfect body creates for him, in the safety of ever-flowing water. The Holy Spirit walks with her in that garden the way God walked with Eve. And in the process of birth, our incarnate God is born through darkness into light by a woman who allows her body to assent to the work of becoming a mother—the Mother of Eternal Life, as Eve was the Mother of All the Living. And with the life of Christ is born the blood and water of the passion, a harbinger of our redemption. The full mystery of our creation and our salvation poured out in the quiet of a Bethlehem stable through the body of a woman.

Can you imagine it? Can there be so great a mystery to follow our creation and our fall as the incarnation that brings about our salvation? Do you feel the rising of the Eden instinct in you, the longing to assent to the beauty of that mystery? How do we respond to a love letter so great and so perfect from our God?

~ ON THE ROAD TO JUDEA WITH MARY ~

When someone offers that kind expression of love to you, there is only one affirmative response to offer in return—to receive that love. And since Mary chose not to reject the love of God, the only response she could offer is one we have come to call her *fiat*, her response to the angel Gabriel: "Let it be done unto me."

Mary, by her immaculate conception, enjoyed a unique intimacy with God that gave her a profound understanding of his will, just as Eve did when she walked in the garden of Eden with him, naked and unashamed. Mary had no need for the fig leaf or the covering of God's mercy for her concupiscence, so she is able to live the ideal relationship of woman living naked and unashamed before God.

What did that look like since clearly Mary's nakedness was not physical? What did it mean for Mary to grow from childhood to adulthood with nothing dividing her from God, with nothing to hide, with no fear of her utter dependence on him, and without any consequences of disobedience to his will?

What was Mary's prayer life like as a child? How did her relationship with God change as she reached adolescence? Was she afraid for Joseph when her betrothal was announced, even though she fully trusted God to prepare him for his role? Did she sense the moment drawing near, much the way Eve knew God was looking for her in the garden that day after she had eaten the apple?

What a beautiful comparison to imagine, that in contrast to looking for a place to hide, when Gabriel's light dawned and his voice sounded, Mary simply stepped forward with nothing to hide, naked in her vulnerable perfection the way woman was meant to be before God. And with her *fiat*, she replaces the moment that Eve asserted her own will in the place of God's, with perfect assent, body and soul, intellect and will, overcoming fear, the risk of persecution and unknowing, to stand naked before God and offer herself to him as slave, servant, bride, and mother.

Mary, while perhaps not surprised by the angel's announcement, questioning only to confirm the details of how the event would unfold, does seem to quicken with a surprised joy at the knowledge that her cousin Elizabeth, so long thought barren, is now not only pregnant, but advanced in her pregnancy. Mary, the gospel tells us, felt a need to make haste to her.

The Bible does not tell us if Mary packed up her things before leaving, if she spoke to anyone, if she went alone or joined a traveling caravan. We only know that she went in haste, her spirit quick to know that in the first moments of the incarnation, as soon as her "be it done unto me" was spoken, she was meant to be on her way to the moment of her Magnificat, where she proclaimed God's greatness in what he had done in her for all of creation.

If Mary did indeed walk alone to Elizabeth and Zechariah's home, it is likely she had five dusty days on foot, walking nearly the entire day, to ponder just how the interchange between her and her beloved had happened and what came next. It is also likely her eyelids grew heavy with the exhaustion of early pregnancy and her mouth grew dry more quickly than normal. I wonder if she found shady spots to nap or stopped at warm inns along the way to seek refuge from the cold, desert night wind. Did she speak to anyone? Try to pretend all was normal, carry on casual conversation while God was being pieced together cell by cell inside her body? Or did she, as it seems she spent so much of her life doing, simply ponder it all in her heart?

I'm guessing she spent much of her travel time alone, communing with the God who now not only walked with her but dwelled in her, praying for the salvation of the world to come, praying for our yes, hoping that we would echo her *fiat* and become the new generation of Eves behind her, the women who would push away the desire to assert our wills and instead assent to God in willing and joyful servitude.

When she finally arrives on Elizabeth's doorstep, there is the moment for speech, for conversation, for celebration. Finally, in the hands of a friend who gets the depth of the spiritual experience she has had, Elizabeth's bulging belly and aged hands reach for Mary's still secret womb and youthful cheeks as she feels the joy of salvation inside her own body, and Mary releases its hope into the world for the first time.

The scene in the Gospel of Luke says Mary entered the house and greeted Elizabeth. I imagine Elizabeth at the fire in the back corner of the house, or resting on a mat of straw, her face turned to a corner and Mary walking quietly through the door and calling her name. And Elizabeth startling as the babe in her womb leaps in recognition, and then she too leaps up, that the salvation her little one was prophesied to proclaim has come, is here in her home in the womb of the most blessed of women, our beautiful Mary.

When Elizabeth and her babe recognize God present in Mary's womb and proclaim with wonder and joy the blessing that it is to them he has first come, when Mary can feel with certainty that now is the time and this is the moment and she will no longer be the only one to know it, what else is left to but proclaim her love of the Lord?

She who has reversed the assertion of Eve with her own assent and become woman once again united to God in consummate love responds to his love letter to humanity, his incarnation and our salvation, with her own love song, the song we call the Magnificat.

Imagine Mary as she stands before Elizabeth in the quiet shadows of a simple home in Judea, John the Baptist squirming with the delight of salvation in his mother's womb, and Mary knowing the life in her own womb is who he said he would be, this song escaping from her lips: "My soul magnifies the Lord and my spirit rejoices in God my Savior, because he has looked with favor on the lowliness of his servant...and done great things for me, and holy is his name" (Luke 1:46–49).

The new Eve's life from this point forward becomes a constant movement back and forth from *fiat* to Magnificat, from assent to God's will to consummate love of the Lord, from "be done unto me" to "my soul magnifies the Lord, holy is his name." Mary's life becomes the path for all of us back to Eden, the path to accept the salvation that will bring us back to eternal union with God. Mary's *fiat* is her nakedness of dependence before the Lord, and her Magnificat is her unashamed love for him.

Her yes opens the path for us to embrace that same life and re-member ourselves to God through the body of Christ here on earth, the Church.

~ SURRENDERED TO GRACE ~

We the daughters of Eve, who have inherited both the *imago dei* in the feminine form and the propensity to assert our passions where we are meant to assent with our will in obedience to God, become also the daughters of the new Eve, Mary, spouse of the Holy Spirit, Immaculate Conception, queen of Heaven and Earth, and mother of the Christ, whose bride is the Church.

This, my friends, is cause for rejoicing because it is in "membering" ourselves to the Church, the bride and body of

Christ, that we re-member who we are and revive the Eden instinct that pulls us back together, body and soul, to be the women God created us to be when he was writing us as a love letter to himself.

If sin is our fall, and the way our bodies and souls disintegrate, body aligning with passions and disconnecting from our will and intellect, then grace is our way to be re-membered or put back together. The sacramental grace of the Church is the bodily, tangible way we become whole again. Surrendering to that grace is the way we echo the *fiat* yes and Magnificat proclamation of God's generosity with our Mother Mary, so that we can stand once again naked and unashamed with our first mother, Eve.

Traditionally in the Church, we have defined the sacraments as "visible signs of inward grace." In other words, if we choose to cooperate with the grace they offer, the sacraments become tangible, bodily signs of an action occurring within our souls that is leading us closer to Christ, uniting us more fully to the Church, and leading us to eternal life.

The Church, in all her wisdom, knows that God created us as bodily creatures and that the most important aspects of our faith, the ones that touch the greatest mysteries of how we unite ourselves to God, must be bodily experiences as much as they are spiritual ones. The Church, following the example of a Savior who healed with spit and dirt and then proclaimed it was faith that had saved, does not separate our physical experience of grace from our spiritual experience of it.

The Church understands our human makeup, body and soul, and knows our Eden instinct longs for both aspects of our selves to come back to the fullness of our original relationship with

God. So she pours water on our heads and anoints us with oil, she places us in front of a flesh and blood man that we might receive the words of forgiveness for our sins, and she takes the bread and wine in obedience to Christ's command, transfigures it into his actual flesh, and places it on our lips for us to consume.

The ultimate act of union we can have with God this side of heaven is our communion with him in the Eucharist, and it is a literal fleshly experience of consuming his body into our own, receiving the grace to remember ourselves as Eve, naked before him, dependent on him for our sustenance, and in total assent to his will.

As we open ourselves to receive Christ in the Eucharist, we urge our hearts to the same cooperation that Mary offered the Holy Spirit, a *fiat*, a "be it done unto me." We stand wide open before our God to receive him into ourselves and accept that our work is then to believe in that reception with enough faith that our life becomes a Magnificat song of proclaiming his goodness and faithfulness to us in our lowliness.

Grace is the center point on our seesaw life between being made in the image of God and being able to deny him in sin. Grace brings order to the two sides of our Edenic and sinful nature and brings our soul back into union with itself inside our bodies so that both can then reflect that spiritual harmony.

In Eden, before sin, Eve lived in harmony with God, his creation, Adam, and herself. The spiritual integration for us as women today would be to live in perfect assent to the will of God, care for his creation, be at peace with our neighbor, and fully connect to ourselves body and soul. Sin destroys that harmony, but Mary makes it possible for us to remember and long for it by consenting to the incarnation of our God inside her, giving us a path to our salvation. As we await that salvation on earth, the sacraments impart the grace we need to find and reclaim what we can of that Eden harmony and cooperate more fully with the will of God so that we can live a life of physical and spiritual integration that mimics the life of Eden as closely as can be lived this side of heaven.

The first sacraments of the Church—baptism, Communion, and confirmation—are called the sacraments of initiation. They literally re-member us to the body of Christ and make it possible for us to remember our Eden selves through grace. In baptism, we are washed in the waters, like the rivers that flowed through Eden and fed the garden's fruitfulness, in order to be freed from the stain of original sin that makes harmony with God impossible for us. We are welcomed bodily into his body, the Church, and invited to live once again in harmony with him. Clothed in white, we are a symbol of a new life, naked and without shame. We are made new and transformed, brought back to our Eden identities, made once again like God.

Over time, our newly baptized innocence must come face-to-face with the other half of the inheritance Eve left us, our sinful natures. While our bodies have often been focused on as the locus of that sin, the truth is that all sin comes from a disorder within our souls, the place where our will and intellect cannot overcome the desires of our passions and we follow them into disobedience to God. Much like Eve, we eventually let desire convince us that the sinful thing we want is actually good and that God would want us to have it. Often the pleasure we gain is a carnal one, a bodily pleasure. But it is not our bodies where our sinful desires originate. St. Paul's frequent reference to "the flesh" as that part of us that tempts away from obedience to God is not a reference, as many think, to our physical bodies, but to the locus of our passions at the lowest level of our souls.

The sacrament of reconciliation is the process by which one man in one body, the priest, brings us back into harmony with God and ourselves through the forgiveness of our sins so that we can be reunited also to the body of Christ, the Church. The sacrament of forgiveness is the sacrament of restoration of our Eden-endowed harmony. What beauty to know that each time we destroy our *fiat* of assent to God by consuming Satan's lies, we can be returned to the Magnificat proclamation of God's great mercy through the bodily act of absolution, which removes the fig leaf of shame from our bodies and souls, and sends us back out into the world covered in God's merciful love.

In confirmation, we assume before the Church Mary's posture before the angel Gabriel. We stand open-armed as members of the bride of Christ and allow the Holy Spirit to overshadow us too. We surrender ourselves to the gifts and graces he delights to bestow on us, and promise to use those gifts for the good of our own bodies and souls as well as the body of the Church. We are restored to the harmony of Eden in the community in which we live, at the disposal of one another for the good of all.

Then, daily God comes again in the bread and wine so that we might receive his body and blood into our very own bodies. He takes the single bone of our beginning and layers himself over all the places his image in us has been damaged, mending the tears we have wrought in the way he knit us together with the gift of grace so that we might live in him and him in us. We don't undo Eden's fall by dressing ourselves in God, covering what was undone with our shame. We undo it by gradually relearning what it is to consummate ourselves in love to our God, commune with him, body and soul, and let that communion bring us to a life that surrenders easily to the waves of "let it be done" and "my soul proclaims his greatness." This is the way an incarnate God brings salvation to the children he created in love. This is the signature of the love letter he wrote when he put on skin as Jesus our Redeemer. And it leads us, in our surrender, to the door of eternity, where one day he will delight to pick us up and carry us over the threshold in the fullness of Eden love with him.

Mary walks beside us as mother and guides with her gentle hand, teaching us the constant responses of her *fiat* and Magnificat, and Eve stands out before us, beckoning us back to the paradise of Eden that is now the eternal life of heaven, where we have the possibility to live as she did, naked and unashamed in the garden of our God.

~ SHANNON'S STORY ~

The tattoo artist cocked her head, lost in thought, clearly trying to imagine the picture I brought her tattooed on my arm. Yet I had begun making plans for this the first time I laid eyes on the art print of Mary and Eve drawn by a sister of Our Lady of the Mississippi Abbey. The two women stand face-to-face, Eve, covered only in her long dark hair, holding an apple in one hand and touching Mary's pregnant belly with the other. Mary's hand outstretched, cupping Eve's face with all the shocking tenderness we're convinced she doesn't deserve.

But it was the bottom of the picture that stole my heart. A long green serpent is wrapped hauntingly around Eve's calf. Mary's foot peeks out from under her blue robe, stepping meekly yet triumphantly on the head of the snake.

And just like that, the story of humanity's redemption is told by two women.

I became Catholic at thirty years old and my road of faith had taken some twists and turns in the three decades prior. Most were the years I bought into the lie that heaven was more important than earth, that miracles were greater than physical substance, and I became numb to the thousands of ways that God lives and moves and has his being through the tangible, sensory stuff of earth.

But a season of doubt and suffering delivered grace and eyes to see my faith in new ways. The sacramental nature of the Catholic Church drew me like a magnet to her love of all things physical. Whether it was smelling the incense, hearing an absolution, tasting the Eucharist, kneeling, genuflecting, seeing Christ incarnated in the poor, or contemplating the very fact that Jesus took on flesh like mine, I couldn't escape the million proofs of a Creator's delight in creation nor his determination to use it to woo me on earth.

I began to see that the intent of Christ was never to relegate redemption to the spiritual realm, leaving us to wait desperately to shed this cumbersome physical world. No, he is in all things and he holds everything together. He is in the bread we eat, he is in the touch of our neighbor, he is in the tears of our children, he is in the dirt we dig up, and he is in the voice of the poor.

In the picture now etched onto my skin, Eve represents the me that has tried to run and hide from the physical realm. She is ashamed, waiting out the redemption, waiting for the day when all things are made new and she can finally enter into the glory that awaits her. The snake still has its perilous hold.

But Mary speaks of my physicality. I cannot look at Mary's swollen figure and forget that our God embraces the earth. Mary crushes the head of the liar, and I remember again what the Good News is. Redemption has already begun; it pulses through sunlight and tattooed arms.

~ FURTHER UP AND FURTHER IN ~

Were you baptized as a baby or an adult, or somewhere in between? Do you have any memories of that day? Today, light a candle and bless yourself with holy water, remembering your baptism and imaging yourself literally being put back together, body and soul, and made part of the body of the Church.

What is your relationship with the Eucharist like? How do you feel when you receive the Body of Christ, before, during, after? If you have never considered it, at your next reception, make note of the bodily sensations you feel in each of those stages and journal about it at your next prayer time.

What has been your experience of the sacrament of reconciliation? We all have good stories and bad stories. But do you think there is importance to making the forgiveness we receive for our sins physical in some way? What evidence is there in the gospels that Jesus knows we need to be touched in physical ways to comprehend how faith heals us? Try reading the following passages for ideas: John 9:1–11, Mark 7:31–37, Matthew 20:29–33

Consider your own relationship with Mary. Who is she to you? Who has she been? What role do you wish she would play more of in your life?

CHAPTER FOUR

⸺✸⸺

THE DEARTH AND DEPTH

True Talk About Self Care

He saw from the roof a woman bathing; and the woman
was very beautiful.

—2 SAMUEL 11:2

Now she was purifying herself after her period.

—2 SAMUEL 11:4

When the wife of Uriah heard that her husband was dead,
she made lamentation for him. When the mourning was
over, David sent and brought her to his house, and she
became his wife, and bore him a son.

—2 SAMUEL 11:26–27

· · · · ·

Around the time of my forty-third birthday, I was having
lunch with a dear friend. As we sat sipping mojitos on
the sunlit patio of our favorite restaurant in the small
Costa Rican town where we live, the words spilled from my
mouth about how tired I was and how I was unsure how to
recover from the burnout I was feeling. She leaned in, took
my hand, and with her famously empathetic eyes asked, "Can
this be the year we take care of you?" I shied away from the

intimacy of the question and the answer I knew I needed to give. See, this friend is a midwife, and while the habit we had made of sneaking away when we could for lunch and a cocktail was renewing and fulfilling for both of us, I knew she meant more than that when she said "care." She is a woman whose life is dedicated to the holistic care of other women. I knew the request for self-care she was holding out to me was way deeper than the paper cocktail umbrellas and pedicured toes the world tries to sell us women as self-care.

But I am pretty sure she never imagined the day she would calm me on the phone after an irregular mammogram, the day she would see the reality of what I meant by severe anxiety and self-harm tendencies, what she would come to know about the roots and depths of my pain and shame. And I know for a fact she never imagined the day she would hold my head in her lap in the back of our car as we drove to the office of the psychiatrist who would admit me to the hospital for a nervous breakdown. But she didn't back away when those moments came, because when she said, "Take care of yourself," she meant my whole self.

See, these are the things no one wants to talk about when we start the conversation with women about self-care. There is an entire market building around the concept and seemingly endless varieties of "care" available for us to claim for ourselves. But where the consumer world lacks understanding is where women of spirit, women aware that they are body and soul, must stand up and fight for a new definition of self-care, one that focuses more on the fullness of self than on easy answers about what "care" could look like. We are not one-dimensional beings who can be shined up in ways that can be paid for with the swipe of our flat plastic cards

The question we need to give ourselves permission to ask is not how to feel better, freer, recognized, heard, or seen for a moment over a coffee date or a spa massage, but how to feel whole and genuinely loved inside the skin of our bodies and the depths of our souls—intellect, will, and passions. This is the form God gave us when he created us in his image in Eden and individualized for each of us when he knit us together stitch by cellular stitch in our mothers' wombs. It is complex, layered, relational, and constantly developing. And we are the only ones who fully understand what it means to be ourselves and what those selves need. The great and grand mystery of who we are and what is required to care for us lies primarily in the process of self-discovery we can only embark upon if we follow our Eden instinct back to harmony with God and ourselves. It is a challenging journey, but one worth saying yes to, because knowing who we were when we lived naked and without shame is the only way to know who we want to be when we are well cared for and whole again.

The challenge that remains after that journey is equally daunting. It is the challenge to give ourselves permission to need on a grander and deeper scale than the world would like us to. As women, we are constantly imbibing the contradictory message that we are all at once not enough and too much. It leaves us feeling that however we voice the reality of who we are and what we need, we are somehow wrong. This self-judgment heaps shame upon the nakedness we have risked to reveal our true selves and their deepest needs.

And the truth is, there *are* those who would vilify the nakedness of our need and our attempts to meet it—who would judge us for the choices we make in caring for ourselves and declare them all wrong, not spiritual enough, too medicalized, too selfish, silly, or any other manner of things that would make it seem easier for us to put our fig leaves of shame back on and make our way into the bushes to hide our nakedness.

But let us not give in and ignore the Eve inside us and her longings for the harmony in which we were meant to live. Let us not abandon the hope of permission to know and recognize our whole selves and care for them, even if it looks a little messy, kind of ugly, or slightly selfish to the outside world. Let us revolutionize the world of self-care by converting it from a consumer fad to a spiritual awakening of feminine wholeness that has the power to change us and the world in which we live for the better. No one else is able to decide for us who we are and what we need; we can only find ourselves in the God who created us. The cornerstone of every step we take to care for ourselves must be trust in his great love for us.

~ CONSIDERING THE NATURE OF SELF ~

The major issue in the dearth of true self-care options for us as women in the world today is a reluctance to dig to the depths of what the self really is and means. We are sold the idea that we are made of mind, body, and spirit, and that these are the aspects of self we should be attentive to in order to find ourselves healthy and whole, in other words, cared for. In addition to that, most efforts want to skim the surface of these three areas, focusing on time for ourselves, physical exercise, a few sensory indulgences, and some creative outlet to stimulate us mentally. While each of these things may, in fact, end up playing a role in our efforts at true self-care, it is important for us to consider that all of these solutions are based in a faulty, half-complete definition of self.

In the Catholic faith, we are not creatures made of mind, body, and spirit; we are creatures made of body and soul. That soul has a three-part hierarchy of intellect, will, and passions. And it goes even deeper than that. St. Thomas Aquinas created a full diagram of the make-up of the human person that assigns us three categories of powers, with a total of ten sub-categories which are then divided further into twenty-three more defined aspects of thought, knowledge, and appetites.[5] This book includes a diagram of these categories on p. 190. In short, understood through the lens of God's creative magnitude and the Church's age-old knowledge of the human condition, the self is a complex, multi-layered being whose needs could be innumerable. Add to that reality the historical, and likely correct, interpretation that women have a deeper awareness of and feel those levels of self more acutely, and we must make a mental shift in our portrayal of "self" if we are ever to get to the heart of self-care.

We return to the creation story and consider God holding in his hand that one strong rib of Adam and layer by layer forming woman, with the normal animal powers of reproduction, growth, and nutrition; then the appetites or passions of her senses; the knowledge those senses can acquire for her; then the rational powers of her intellect and will. And then consider that all that layering and complexity was singularly ordered toward the capacity to give and receive love—first to God, then self, others, and creation. This is the Eden harmony for which woman was created. This is the female self. Each element of the complex mystery of womanhood plays a distinct role in allowing us to love fully and thus live fully.

Thomas Merton says in *New Seeds of Contemplation*, "In our creation, God asked a question, and in our truly living, God answers the question." The question, it seems, is based in our ability to love and God's desire to be loved by us. "Will you love me?" God asks as he creates us, and our lives become the response to that question, animated not by our own ability to love but in the way he created us to love, by giving us the opportunity to reveal the answer with our free will, each in our own way.

Self-care becomes the habit of taking account of where we are on the spectrum of all these complex aspects of how we are made and what we need to do to order them more fully toward loving God so that we can better love ourselves and others. There was a popular Christian phrase that was tossed around in my youth group years ago that claimed that the definition of true JOY was to think about Jesus first, then Others, then Yourself. While that trite acronym may have served some purpose toward overcoming the ego-focused phase of adolescence, it seems to have been imbued in Catholic culture in a way that many of us carried it with us wholeheartedly into womanhood with guilt attached to the inevitable reality of being needy humans.

The truth is that God never intended us to live the harmony he created at Eden in a linear way, always ordered in only one direction, with any variance in that relational line breaking the rules of being Godlike. We are made to be relational beings who are quite capable of giving and receiving fully all at once—to God, to others, *and* to ourselves. We are in no one way obligated by God to put ourselves in last place, scraping for the crumbs of his goodness and compassion and pretending we are full while we are really starving to death. We are capable of giving to ourselves in ways that go to the deepest mysteries of who we are and how we are created, whether it is by caring for our physical body, caring for our mental and emotional health in the ways we need to be stable, rational, and clear in our minds, or caring for the parts of our soul that need attention in order for us to pursue holiness. I firmly believe that when it comes to how he designed the complexity of self, God trusted us to understand that holiness would by its nature include wholeness, and that he delights in our efforts to understand our human natures and care for them in the way he would have in Eden, so that every need of ours is met.

If we return to Merton's assumption that God asked a question in the way he created each of us individually, and that question is answered by our living fully, then the truth is self-care becomes not optional but imperative in our quest to live as God created us to live, to follow our longings back to our Eden instinct.

Merton continues in *New Seeds of Contemplation* with this thought: "Our vocation is not simply to be, but to work together with God in the creation of our own life, our own identity, our own destiny....to work out our identity in God." If it is, in fact, our vocation as women not simply to exist as created beings, but to work together with God to create our lives and our identities, then a radical commitment to understanding the layers and levels of ourselves and knowing how to care for them, is, in fact, a necessary part of being human.

The beauty of using St. Thomas Aquinas's complex assessment of what "self" means rather than opting for the ever popular but overly simple "mind body spirit" approach is this: It frees us as women from the assumption that we are *supposed to* loathe our bodies. Over and over in Scripture, we hear sinful things being referred to as "of the flesh," and we are taught that "carnal" things are wrong. The truth is, it is our passions—located in our souls, not our bodies—that lead us to sin, and then only when those passions become disordered and lead us away from God and toward evil when they are created to do the opposite.

The beautiful reality behind this complexity is that you can trust that your body, capable as it may be of following your disordered passions into sin, is not in and of itself a shell of concupiscence that is out to do you in as you attempt to live a godly, Eden-inspired life. Your body is your friend and your tool and can become your trustworthy guide toward holiness rather than away from it!

And the beautiful truth underlying that reality is that the more confidence you place in understanding your entire spiritual and physical self, layer by layer, the more capable you will become of a self-care that is honoring to God, to yourself, and to others, not one before the other, but all at once, in the Eden harmony that is yours to claim.

~ On the Roof with Bathsheba ~

It was spring in Jerusalem, the time when kings march out to war. King David was, in fact, ready to follow suit and send his troops out to "destroy the Ammonites and besiege Rabbah" (2 Samuel 11:1). They were, it seems, having easy success in both efforts. But King David himself had not gone out to war with his troops as the custom seems to imply was his duty. For the verse goes on to say that he had "stayed back in Jerusalem" (2 Samuel 11:1).

Who knows what it was that kept David in Jerusalem instead of marching out to war beside his troops as duty seemed to prescribe. Perhaps it was that spring in Jerusalem is fleeting and undeniably pleasant to the senses, covered in the loveliness of pink almond blossoms and unpredictable weather that can be cool one day and then warmer the next for just a few short weeks.

Maybe there were kingly things to be done at that palace that did not allow him to leave for war with his troops. Whatever the reason may be that David found himself in the palace instead of the battlefield the day he placed his lustful eyes on Bathsheba, we do know this much: He was not distracted from dutiful service by her, as so often it is made to seem when this story is recounted. The Scriptures instead have David "getting up from bed and strolling on the roof of the palace in the evening" (2 Samuel 11:2).

It is easy to imagine a powerful king like David, home with no troops to manage, rising from an afternoon siesta of sorts and stretching himself awake by heading up to the roof on a seasonably warm evening to take a stroll and enjoy the view of Jerusalem such a palace undoubtedly afforded him. Only what caught his eye was not that view, but the body of a beautiful woman bathing on a nearby rooftop, the body of Bathsheba, the wife of Uriah the Hittite, a faithful soldier in David's army (2 Samuel: 2–3).

So why was Bathsheba bathing on the roof in plain sight? Later in this story, we are given a side note that she had been bathing to purify herself from the uncleanness after her period. This was not a simple everyday bath that Bathsheba had decided to enjoy on the roof simply so she could be naked out in the open where anyone could see her.

The *mikveh* that Jewish women undertook when their bleeding was complete after a menstrual cycle or postpartum period was both a spiritual and physical ritual, an act of self-care prescribed by their faith. Not only did the act of purification apply to the woman herself, but it was considered an act that purified and made clean again her entire family. Consider that concept—an act of ritual self-care of body and soul prescribed by her religion that brought not only the woman but her entire family back into accord with their community. Bathsheba's bath was not selfish, lustful pleasure; it was a sacred rite of her culture and faith.[6]

With her husband Uriah away, and the possibility that he could return at any moment for respite from his battles, Bathsheba purified herself in order to be available to him once again for intercourse in accord with the Jewish law. She was making preparations with that bath to serve Uriah's needs after a long time away at war and offer herself in intimacy to her spouse.

Then there is the issue of the rooftop. According to the ritual law, some of the water used in the bath had to be collected from a natural source: a river, an ocean, or rain water. Considering it was spring, and we all know the fame of unpredictable spring showers, it makes perfect sense that Bathsheba would have placed something on the roof to collect rain water when it did fall, knowing she would need to perform the ritual soon after her period ended. In addition, the law requires that women immerse themselves in the water, not simply wash with it, which would have required Bathsheba's nakedness for the process.

For a moment, imagine what it was like, in a culture where showering daily as we are so accustomed to was not the norm, for Bathsheba to finally be at the end of the misery of her period, a misery we all know too well, to be thankful that it ended before Uriah arrived home, and that she had time for her bath. That it had rained and she had the water she needed, that it was warm and pleasant that spring day on the roof and that the scent of almond blossoms filled the air, and blood-red poppies that mimicked her own body's cycle hung ripe from branches. Maybe she had even floated a few blossoms in her bath water.

I don't know about you, but a warm, cleansing bath during a period may be for me one of the most comforting self-care rituals I offer myself on a regular basis. So I can just feel Bathsheba's relief as she stepped into that sun-warmed water. Perhaps she closed her eyes, tilted her head toward the sky and let her hair fall loose down her naked back, soaking in the comfort of the process. Maybe she moved her lips in the ritual prayers of her people or hummed a pleasant tune to herself as we are prone to do when we bathe and assume we are alone. Maybe she blushed a bit thinking of the intimacy she would share with Uriah when he arrived. Maybe she let the soap linger long down her legs and arms for the sheer pleasure it brought her. And surely there would have been a washing of her most intimate parts, as that was, in fact, the purpose of the bath itself.

Sometimes, I laugh at how good I feel all wet and soapy in the shower, enjoying the sensation of touching my body gently and giving it the gift of cleanness, the nice scent of the shampoo, the relaxation of being surrounded by the warmth of the water and the steam that fills the room. I often laugh again when I step out of the shower to see myself in the mirror only to remember that that woman is me, not the one I imagined myself to be in the shower when I felt sensual and lovely. But if anyone happened to peek through that curtain during my shower, he or she may well assume my actions were meant to entice and lure. I feel, in fact, sexual and sensual, relaxed and relieved, and more comfortable in my skin than most other times throughout the day. I would dare say I am probably most appealing to the outside eye during a bathing ritual, and I do believe my husband might concur, just as David concurred when he spotted Bathsheba in all her beauty there on her rooftop. The only problem was that David was not her husband and had no right to respond to his lust for her, other than the entitlement he enjoyed as king. So he takes what is not his with the misuse of a power God had bestowed on him for his righteousness, and then throughout history, it seems, Bathsheba, rather than him, takes the blame for her nakedness, her practicing of self-care in the way she was not only allowed, but, in fact, obligated to by the laws of her faith.

Bathsheba loses everything in the process. Her husband Uriah is murdered; the child she conceives with David dies seven days after birth. Bathsheba, we are told, mourns Uriah's death before she dutifully returns to David's house to be his wife, since he is the father of her child. As 2 Samuel continues, we are told that it is the death of his son that finally causes David to accept his responsibility for the carnage he has caused. He fasts and weeps in hope that his son's life will be saved, and when death takes the little one, David purifies himself in the ritual way required, mirroring Bathsheba's righteousness in the act that initiated this sad story. It is a redemptive act that turns the course of events around for the good. When David admits his own fault and relieves Bathsheba of her undeserved burden, she, then, is able to forgive and accept David as her husband and bear him the son we all know as King Solomon.

Bathsheba stands naked on the roof the day this story begins, caring for herself. Later, she meets her own needs by taking time to properly mourn the death of her husband. And again she heals her own heart when she allows herself to forgive David and experience the joy of the birth of Solomon and the wise man that child becomes. In truth, this tale is an epic story of a woman's self-care that far too often obscures or vilifies Bathsheba, who is the real heroine. I suspect the reason for that might be that the story begins with her nakedness and her beauty, and we are no longer in Eden where those aspects of a woman are accepted without shame.

~ GIVING OURSELVES PERMISSION TO NEED ~

Far too many of us women battle our bodies as enemy and harbor shame as a faithful, albeit unkind, companion. There is heated battle over our mental and emotional states, about how careful we must be about what we share with others, about how vulnerable and naked we are allowed to be before the world with our thoughts, feelings and questions about what it means to be woman, whole and holy outside of Eden.

The bottom line is that many of us as women feel as though we should have a vague permission from someone to express our needs and seek ways to care for them. Then when we do step out and risk insisting on real, effective self-care for our bodies and souls, we must battle back feelings of guilt for our selfishness, for being needy. Not to mention, there is an entire world, both secular and religious, ready to vilify us for the choices we make when we decide to be naked before them as we seek to peel away our shame and live wholly as ourselves, complicated and needy but true and real.

Again taking inspiration from Merton in *New Seeds of Contemplation*, we have this gem to apply to our pursuit of self-care: "Do not look for rest in any pleasure, because you were not created for pleasure: you were created for spiritual joy. And if you do not know the difference between pleasure and spiritual joy you have not yet begun to live."

The world wants to sell us the pleasure of pedicures and spa days as self-care. Our spiritual natures long for time for prayer, contemplation, and retreat from the stresses of our overpacked daily lives. Our bodies long for rest, rejuvenation, movement, and nourishment. Our senses long for beauty and a connection to the created world. Our emotions long for a place to be released and received without judgment so they can return to their rightful order and bring us closer to God and others.

We have been completely off the mark when it comes to how we define self-care for women. We allow the prescription for our bodily care to be written by the world of marketing that negates us as individuals and sees us as consumers. We confine our need for spiritual care—our need to wrestle out our doubts, our disappointment in God, and the wounds inflicted on the body of Christ—to discussions in quiet voices with a few safe friends, if we can find them. And if our need for emotional and mental health should require more than a listening ear, should need professional support, medication, and a diagnosis, we hide under the veneer of being okay so as not to let people see our spiral into darkness and be accused of lacking faith. We feel boxed in and divvied up all at once, right back to that place of being too much and not enough as women.

If Merton's assertion is true, then we begin to live and experience spiritual joy when we stop trying to separate the physical female experience of who we are from the spiritual female experience of who we are. When we begin to see that God created them to exist together in cohesion, we are brought back into the Eden harmony our hearts long for. This is when we begin to fully live and know spiritual joy.

The root of that cohesion is giving ourselves permission to need. When God created woman in the Garden of Eden, she came with nothing, and it was he who provided all she needed. That utter dependence was a key to the perfection of her relationship with God. It was Eve's decision to attempt to be more like God so that she would not need him so much that became the moment of our fall, the moment we women knew shame for the first time. Throughout history, that shame has clung to our perception of what it is to be needy, to not be able to care for ourselves on our own and without the help of God and others.

But there is no one else who will be the hero or heroine of our self-care story besides us. There is no one who can come out from behind the fig leaf of shame into the nakedness of our need, who can step into that vulnerable state for us. No one else can accept for us that the need to be cared for is part of our nature, part of what makes us long for God, part of the way he made us so that we return the all-encompassing love with which he loves us.

In caring for the full complexity of our God-image stamped selves, we are loving God for the way he made us. In standing naked to announce that, yes, our bodies have forgotten how to feed themselves well and love themselves well and, to our horror and shame, are telling that secret to the world with their forms and shapes, and in admitting that we want so badly to figure out how to care for them well, we are loving God.

In opening up and asking for help when things are not working right in our minds, when synapses are firing in the wrong directions or when trauma has broken some important pathways and life is more complicated than we can figure out on our own, we are loving God.

And in taking a moment or an evening or an entire weekend to make ourselves feel shiny and new, to sip cappuccinos and laugh our silly heads off, to hide in the bathroom to eat dark chocolate, and to finish that much-needed conversation with a friend while we drive around aimlessly, we are loving God.

A radical commitment to self-care is an admittance that we are complex beings made by God and made to need. It is a pledge to ourselves to stand naked and unashamed of those needs, and as long as we maintain the order of our passions and avoid sin, we can give ourselves permission to meet both our bodily and spiritual needs and pursue wholeness without fear.

Are there times we might go overboard and cross the line to selfishness or indulgence or intemperance in the effort? There may be. How do we respond then? We seek mercy from God, and we offer it to ourselves. Truthfully, I think we risk that sin most when we degrade our needs until we are a little more desperate than we should be to meet them. And most often I think the cure for a minor overindulgence in this area is to be gentle with ourselves, knowing that offering ourselves forgiveness and acceptance of our faults may well be the highest level of self-care we can practice. Then we re-member ourselves to the body, the Church, through the sacraments, and reunite our bodies and souls through God's mercy. We take the hand of Mary our mother, who stands open-armed and ready to guide us back into God's will with her gentle love.

Let us give up the fear and shame we carry about needing and remind ourselves that when he layered us together in such complexity, our Father intended for us to be not only needy but fully dependent on him. Outside of Eden, we have to work to meet those needs ourselves as there is no garden to readily offer them up to us, but the desire to have them met is part of our holy Eden longings, and it honors God. We can offer our weary selves to him unashamed of just how much we need to be taken care of, and we can give ourselves permission to understand and meet the needs that come from the depths of us, the deepest places that no one else in the world can see. With the practice of true self-care we give ourselves permission to love those places fully, just as God does and always has, from the moment we were new and fully dependent on him when we were Eve.

~ JESSICA'S STORY ~

While recovering from my most severe nervous breakdown, I often had to refer to a checklist in the morning just to remember to get out of bed.

Making breakfast, showering, getting dressed, brushing my teeth—all seemed foreign, complicated, nearly impossible. I had no idea where to begin, so I'd just lie in bed, paralyzed, and cry. A friend came to my rescue. She didn't ask how she could help. She tucked me into bed and left me to cry while she took care of my kids and brought me meals. When it was time for her to go home, she made me grocery lists, menus, and a simple schedule to follow upon her departure.

According to this schedule, I was allowed to cry for one hour upon waking ("The Hour of Despair" she labeled it), but only one hour. After that I had to get up and go the kitchen and make breakfast. After breakfast, I was to take a hot bath with Epsom salts. Then I had to take a walk and go to work. Look at my writing calendar. Make progress toward deadlines.

She also included a list of gently phrased questions for when my day started to spin out of control and I needed a reminder.

Did you forget your bath?
Have you eaten lunch?
Have you had any water today?
Do you need to take a nap?
Who can you call?

My friend's care—gently insisting that I treat my body and my spirit with the same maternal care that she had—helped me to survive. It was an important step in my healing.

Until my body broke down, I was suspicious of the term "self-care," because it smelled like "self-love," which I believed was the root of all sin. St. Thomas Aquinas himself said so in the *Summa Theologica*. Or so I thought.

Imagine my surprise to find that St. Thomas had his own self-care checklist for overcoming sorrow, and that it looks strikingly like my friend's list, right down to the hot bath. He also says it's good and right to cry: "A hurtful thing hurts yet more if we keep it shut up...whereas if it be allowed to escape...the inward sorrow is lessened." And that we should reach out to friends, meditate on the true and good, and participate in activities that bring us pleasure.

"Charming though it may seem," writes Msgr. Charles Pope, "it is very good advice...we are not simply soul, we are also body. And our bodies and souls interact and influence each other. St Thomas says, 'whatever restores the bodily nature to its due state of vital movement, is opposed to sorrow and assuages it' (I. II ae 38.5)."[7]

After reading, I went back to *Summa Theologica* to find that quote that had troubled me about self-love: "Therefore it is evident that inordinate love of self is the cause of every sin" (Ia–IIae, 77.4). "Inordinate" is the word I needed to examine. When does self-love cross the boundary to self-indulgence? When we inordinately desire something. Even something that might be good for us. Really, it's common sense. When we want something so badly we are willing to do what violates God's will and/ or human reason to get it, our self-love is inordinate. But caring for myself as a dear friend would, as a loving parent would— with our ultimate health, healing, and wholeness as the goal—is to care for myself as God intends.

~ FURTHER UP AND FURTHER IN ~

What were your impressions of the story of David and Bathsheba before this chapter? Have they changed? Read the beginning of 2 Samuel and see if you can find any new insights there.

Study the diagram in the appendix, the one that St. Thomas Aquinas used to explain the self. What does it tell you about how we are made and what our needs might be?

How have you viewed self-care in the past? What are some of your normal self-care routines? What are some self-care dreams you have that you have never met?

What parts of yourself do you give the least attention to? What commitment might you make to care for yourself more in that area?

CHAPTER FIVE

In Pursuit of Joy

Senses and Sensibilities

She...
    ...works with willing hands.
She is like the ships of the merchant,
    she brings her food from far away.
...And provides food for her household.

—Proverbs 31:13–15

She makes herself coverings;
    her clothing is fine linen and purple.

—Proverbs 31:22

She girds herself with strength
    and makes her arms strong.
...
She opens her hand to the poor,
    and reaches out her hands to the needy.

—Proverbs 31:17, 20

Strength and dignity are her clothing,
    and she laughs at the time to come.
She opens her mouth with wisdom,
    and the teaching of kindness is on her tongue.

—Proverbs 31:25–26

. . . . .

The morning we left for the mission field in Costa Rica nearly six years ago, it was, by anyone else's standard, the middle of the night. At around four o'clock in the morning, we stumbled into the airport with five sleepy-eyed little boys and twelve suitcases. Along to help were a friend and his sons. Our first check-in crisis was that the second suitcase for each person we thought was free allowance, was, in fact, charged for. The second was that many of our bags were considerably overweight. What commenced was a madness that no one should have to endure that early in the morning at such a stressful time.

As we opened suitcases and decided what to leave behind, the fact that I was the only woman in the group became quickly evident in the priority items we chose. The men lifted a large blue vintage Ball mason jar, certain it could stay behind.

"Nope," I said firmly, "that goes."

My husband raised his eyebrow. "It's for the laundry detergent," I answered firmly.

Later, they lifted out blank silver paint cans, which for the moment were filled with kids' underwear.

"These?" they asked.

I shook my head. Those were for utensils in the kitchen and art supplies in the homeschooling area.

And so it continued, those men holding up all the little bits of beauty I had so carefully chosen to make space for in our humble new life, and me shaking my head no to their being left behind.

I knew we were headed for some of the hardest months of our lives. We had to adjust to a new place, a new culture, a new language, a new climate. We were still grieving so many losses in the recent years in our own lives, not to mention the grief of leaving behind a community of friends who loved and supported us. It was going to be my job to make that place feel like home for five bereft and confused little boys as they transitioned, and to tend my own heart as well, plus to do the work that would enable my husband to get this mission going so we could all soon enjoy serving the people we were headed to serve.

With that expectation placed squarely on my shoulders, I knew I needed to bring beauty to the task and create joy for our family by filling our surroundings with things that looked, felt, or smelled lovely.

Seeking beauty is the pathway to seeking joy, and as women, we are endowed with unique gifts that allow us not only to long for that joy that is a reflection of our longing for heaven, but to create and birth things that are noble, good, and lovely in unique and creative ways. We see beyond the material pursuit of simple sensual pleasure to the longing for joy that points our eyes and hearts toward the eternal. St. John Paul II names sensitivity as part of his concept of the feminine genius—the unique gifts women bring to the world by their very nature. While his focus was on the idea that women can see beyond the exterior surface into the interior needs of people and circumstances, I think there is also considerable evidence that part of the gift of sensitivity is women's ability to know that beauty and creativity lift both ordinary experiences as well as the deepest joys and sorrows of life to a higher level, a level that brings a bit of eternal hope to the people around them. We appreciate the privilege of being alive in a world that yields such beauty not only to pleasure our senses, but to bring us true joy by drawing near to our Creator through his creation and the creativity with which he has endowed us.

When God placed the finished Eve in Eden, his desire was for her to enjoy the fruits of the garden, the rivers that ran through it, and the animals that inhabited it. I am quite certain in her nakedness and lack of shame, she did so with a pleasure in her senses those of us who live in concupiscent bodies will never quite be able to allow ourselves to enjoy. Eve could trust her desires and passions because she walked with God in an unbroken union that protected her from experiencing those pleasures in a disordered way, until that moment when she chose her own desire over God's will.

For us, her daughters, it is true that while we are made to long for beauty and the enjoyment of created things with our senses, our fallen nature's passions and desires can all too easily overcome the order by which these pleasures must be measured, and we can find ourselves, as Eve did, consuming those things we are not meant to consume or overindulging in ways that compel us away from the good of God rather than toward it. It is this disorder of our passions and desires that turns our natural Eden longing for the joy and ecstasy of experiencing all of creation with holy desire into sin rather than closeness with God.

That possibility can make us as women, in all our sensitivity, afraid of the pleasures of our senses and can block our pursuit of honest joy and creativity. We become wary of our ability to properly enjoy the things of this world like food, clothing, shopping, the company of others, and even a good fine wine without questioning ourselves and where that line is between desiring the goodness of things to know joy and desiring them to an extent that draws us into ourselves and away from God.

The Church has a long history of understanding the concupiscent human person and his or her struggles in the pursuit of holiness. She believes, for sure, in the need for beauty and things pleasing to our senses. She gives artists and creatives a place of honor in her history. But she also knows our nature's tendency to easily slip into disordered desires and choose sensual pleasures in place of the lasting joy that pulls us toward heaven, so she has created a guidebook to help us navigate our senses and order them toward the goodness of God. That guide consists of the virtues, their meanings, and the Church's encouragement to cultivate them in our lives. When we practice—and practice we must because we will surely be imperfect in our efforts—the virtues, we learn to keep our sensual pleasures ordered toward God and away from evil. Virtue becomes the measure that allows us to enjoy freely the beauty of this world we so naturally long for; we can be naked and without shame in the measure to which we desire those things as a pathway to earthly and eternal joy—a longing that we brought along with us when we left Eden behind.

~ Considering Joy and Pleasure ~

In the world, and sometimes even the Church we live in today, women are shouldering the burden of a most perplexing dichotomy—a message that we must shrink to be less while at the same time expanding to be more. We should be thinner, but we should eat every delicious item presented to us in stores, restaurants, and Pinterest recipes. "Make all the cupcakes!" the world seems to tell us, "but don't eat so many you get a belly bulge or a big butt." We are told to accept our own beauty and be confident in who we are, and then almost immediately all kinds of techniques to plump our lips and lengthen our lashes become all the rage in fashion trends.

There is truth in the thought that God designed us to take pleasure in the sensory world he created—to enjoy that piece of cake, to like your lips (plain or slathered with just the right red) and to know that it is not your job to either shrink or expand, but only to live a life pleasing to the Lord. But it is *not true* that God designed us to live our physical lives primarily for sensory pleasures we can experience inside our bodies. God made us for joy. In a world where many women are being hailed as truth-tellers for being honest about their battles with their bodies and then arriving at the conclusion that the God who loves them simply wants them to do the things that make them feel good, the distinction is important. Recognizing this distinction allows us to find the balancing point where we can freely enjoy the physical pleasures of life without the wariness of our female bodies that often plagues us. It is the difference between enjoying a good meal with friends that reminds us that God is indeed present in our world and good to us, and eating everything that pleases our senses without restraint. One feeds our body and soul, the other feeds our body while it diminishes our soul.

Joy is one of the gifts of the Holy Spirit described in the book of Galatians (5:22–23). If we look at the roots of the words *joy* and *pleasure*, we find a slight but profound difference in their origins. *Joy* has its roots in *gaudere*, meaning "to rejoice," and its earliest English uses were associated with "the source of pleasure or delight," whereas *pleasure* is based in the root *plaisir* ("to please or give pleasure"). We find here that joy, gifted to us by the Holy Spirit, is our ability to rejoice in the source of our pleasure or delight, while pleasure is simply the act of being pleased by something at a sensory level.

We must note the difference and ingrain it on our hearts if we are to understand at all how our bodies and spirits come together into an integrated entity that points us toward God. Holiness does not come from a sour stoicism that snubs its nose at the pleasures of this world and denies the body all pleasure. But neither does it come from a permission to follow the desires of the body wherever they may lead, regardless of the will of God imprinted on our souls and enacted by our intellect and will.

Thinking about the diagram of the human person in our Appendix, what we see about our desires and passions is that they are meant to lead us toward God and away from evil. The reversal of that order is sin. Joy is the way the Holy Spirit guides our passions toward God and measures them with our intellect and will so that we can be confident as we enjoy pleasurable, earthly experiences. When the pleasure directs our hearts toward the source of that pleasure, God, the giver of all good things, and not simply toward earthly desires filled by something that feels, looks, smells, or tastes good, we experience joy in the integration of our physical and spiritual selves. We are not commanded by God to live a life of deprivation because our bodies cannot be trusted. We are commanded to receive from him a life of joy that allows us to use our bodies to rejoice in him as the source of all good things.

One evening, after fighting a heavy anxiety attack that prevented me from attending Mass with my family, I fell into one of those naps that leaves you uncertain of who you are and where you are when you wake up. I had spent the afternoon wrestling with the Lord about a situation that, in my opinion, he should have stepped in and resolved with ease if he truly was good, loved me, and wanted what was best for me. I cried a lot and then spiraled into deep anxiety that left me unable to function for a few hours. But as I came to full awareness after my nap, the first foggy thought to cross my brain was how happy a slice of cake would make me. Since I had spent months eating a diet free of all grains, sugars, and meat, it was an odd thought. And since it was late Sunday evening in rural Costa Rica, when nearly nothing is open, I shook it off as an impossibility.

Not long after, I heard the footsteps of my crew ascending our steps, and my fifteen-year-old son appeared in my doorway holding a small Styrofoam box. "We bought you some cake on the way home from church," he said, nonchalantly. I took that cake and stared at it for a moment, marveling. And then I ate every single sugary bite of it with no regard for my dietary restrictions. I simply enjoyed what was clearly a gift from God. I had spent the better part of an afternoon telling him I was quite sure that I was draped in some kind of invisibility cloak that made him unable to see me in my need. Yes, I loved the cake because it was rich and chocolatey and had sprinkles on top and tasted beyond good. But my enjoyment went deeper than the pleasure of having eaten cake, to the joy of knowing I had been given a gift from the hand of God to remind me that he sees me—even when my biggest, hardest pains are not resolved in the way and time I would like.

Perhaps all our experiences of bodily or sensory pleasures won't be as obviously engineered by God's hand as my piece of chocolate cake, but I firmly believe that if we are women who pray, and pray often, to the Holy Spirit, we will be able to come to know the difference between things that are bringing us earthly pleasure and things that are bringing us joy that draws our heart to God. We can come to trust our bodies if we discipline our spirits and "waste time" with God, or, as a dear spiritual mentor suggested to me, we can let ourselves be wooed by God.

When we talk about returning to our Eden instinct, our hope is to arrive at a point where we are able to stand naked and unashamed before God. When it comes to pleasures surrounding food, drink, exercise, dancing, makeup, clothes, decorating our homes, friendships, and relationships with the opposite sex, it is a difficult task to wade through the gunk the world has clouded that instinct with. Shame is laid upon us from both sides; the command to shrink and the command to expand both cause us to feel as though it is impossible to please everyone and therefore impossible to please anyone, including God.

But the truth is this: God's spirit is moving in you, and he is leaving gifts at the door of your heart. One of those gifts is joy, the gift that will allow you to gauge your desire and satisfy yourself only with that which satisfies him. The key is to train your heart to tone down the world's noise and to look at life through the lens of eternity rather than smoggy clouds of the world's pollution. As you come to know the Holy Spirit better, you will come to know yourself better, and in that knowledge, you will come to trust yourself—and your body—more deeply.

That way of eating I mentioned earlier, that seems in such contrast to my cake experience, is not much different really. I have the great gift of a fantastic, and cheaply priced, masseuse where I live, who truly has healing hands and a prayerful spirit that she uses while she works out the tension in every inch of my body. Whenever it is time to roll over face up during a massage, I take the time to ask my now quiet and relaxed body what it needs from me that I am not giving it. One day, it simply said, "Feed me well, like it is a gift you are giving me." And from that moment, I set aside the excuse that it was easier for me to eat what everyone else was eating, set aside the guilt of needing special foods, set aside the shame of how I had eaten in the past and the inevitable slips to come, and I began to feed my body with the foods I knew made it feel healthiest and most vibrant. It gives me joy to hand out breakfast to my crew and then take a few extra minutes to make my own with the ingredients my body needs. I rejoice in knowing I am caring for myself as God cared for Eve in the garden.

And in both those moments, savoring chocolate cake and eating a nice slab of eggplant covered with sautéed kale and an egg cooked over easy, I am free from shame, able to stand naked before God, knowing that I can rejoice in body and spirit because I am not seeking a momentary pleasure demanded by my desires, but that I am answering my body's desires with the gifts of God's creation in the ordered way he intended, in the way that brings joy to both him and me.

Without a doubt, we will fall and fail at this over and over again. It may well be the hardest aspect of living a healthy relationship between body and soul. But it is so important that we make the effort to grasp it and to pray to the Holy Spirit until we have exhausted our voices. Because knowing the difference between soul joy experienced in the body and bodily pleasure that degrades the soul is the difference between a life of journeying back toward Eden or a life of walking shamefaced away from Paradise.

~ At Home with the Proverbs 31 Woman ~

I titled this section "At Home with the Proverbs 31 Woman" for two reasons: one, she is described as literally working in her home; two, I honestly hope we can let go of our cynicism about this ideal woman and feel more at home with her. For so many women, this Scripture passage has become a measuring stick that yields only one result—a feeling of being an utter failure as a woman and the thought that no matter how hard you try, you will never, ever measure up.

First, let's remember that this passage is advice from Lemuel's mother on choosing a good wife. Rather than seeing the list laid out in Proverbs 31 as a mandatory checklist, perhaps the truth is that his mother was encouraging Lemuel to see a whole host of characteristics that could show the strength and beauty of womanhood, a wide array of feminine goodness he might encounter so he could choose a woman of strength and true beauty who would complement his own kingly strength and authority.

The list provides an opportunity to look at a woman's heart, her longing for beauty and goodness, and to see the many ways we might use the creational aspect of our feminine natures, endowed to us in Eden, to bring beauty to our world. Now, before you put the brakes on this conversation to tell me you do not have a creative bone in your body, and you cannot possibly measure up to the Proverbs woman, let me say this: You were made in the image and likeness of a God who shows off his creativity in grandeur and majesty on a regular basis, and you yourself are of the most splendid examples of that creativity in the history of the created world! Psalm 139 reads "For it was you who formed my inward parts; you knitted me together in my mother's womb. I praise you, for I am fearfully and wonderfully made. Wonderful are your works" (Psalm 139:13–14). First, our God knits! Second, he knitted you together in such a marvelous fashion that when you look at yourself, you should praise him for the wonderful work you are—a marvel of his creative genius. So you do, in fact, as every one of us does, have a creative bone in your body. It is the bone God took in hand and from which created you. Your creativity may not look like someone's perfectly plated dinner party meal or beautifully sewn drapes, but I don't know one woman who is not every day creatively coming up with solutions to save time, money, or energy, balance her life's commitments while still investing in others, and add something lovely to the world around her. This is the creativity we bring to our homes and our lives, whether we are married women or single women, mothers of many or childless, young women or—ahem—more mature women, working out of the home or in the home.

As women, we daily rise to the challenge to meet our responsibilities—often while it is still night—as our eyes sweep open and our brains begin to run the scenarios of the upcoming day and the tasks that lie ahead of us, and we begin to parcel out our time, energy, and resources to tackle those responsibilities in grace, love, and peace. This is exactly what the woman in Proverbs is doing with her time when she "rises while it is still night." Better yet, if you manage to sneak in some time with the Lord, be it short and sweet or a lingering conversation, you are a gem of a woman who knows her days here on earth are fleeting, that this mountain of to-dos is temporary, and that her real righteousness lies in the pursuit of eternal things. You have a value far greater than any precious gem because, morning by morning, you are remembering exactly whose treasure you really are.

Now let's talk about some of the creative things the Proverbs woman is actually doing. First of all, she is procuring and preparing food—gathering things from afar to make good food for the people in her home. Who among us does not enjoy good food? And appreciate our sisters who have a talent for making it? If food is your way to be creative in the caring for others, if planning a menu and scouring for just the right ingredients brings you joy and a sense of purpose, you have a lot in common with the scriptural superwoman. God has given you a creative gift to enjoy food and its preparation. Part of your Eden memory is the wonder of the gorgeous things that grew in that garden and how good it is to prepare, serve, and eat them!

Food is no doubt a creative endeavor that requires a certain amount of desire to bring true joy. None of us can deny that food issues and women seem to be inevitably linked. But the enjoyment of food as a truly joyful experience, free of unhealthy desires or addictions, can bring us contentment and actually be a creative gift with which we serve others and delight God. So if creating delicious and nourishing food is your gift, cook on, and let them praise you at the city gates for its deliciousness.

Here is another fun tidbit about our Scriptural supersister. She likes clothes! She likes to own nice things and wear nice things and make nice things—fine linen and purple being her preference, indicating, in fact, the cultural equivalent of haute couture. She uses her time and resources well, but she does in fact pursue with creative energy the clothes that dress her body beautifully. While we all know how easy it is to fall into bad habits about shopping, or spending resources we do not have, many of us also know all too well the feeling that it is somehow selfish or not virtuous to desire nice things for ourselves. God created Eve naked, so we cannot exactly call this clothes thing an Eden instinct, but the joy we feel as we delight in ourselves and our physical reality when we put on a pretty dress "just because" or find the perfectly fitting pair of jeans peels away the shame many of us have heaped on our bodies. We discover that we can fully enjoy these bodies, just as they are right now, as marvels of creation. That kind of love of looking nice, using your resources wisely to search out just the right item, and taking great delight when you do, is a joy inspired by your innate creativity and appreciated by your Creator, who sees and rejoices when you have found yourself to be wonderfully made. Never feel obligated to hide your imperfect body behind the shame of an ugly and ill-fitting fig leaf!

The woman described in Proverbs 31 is strong, knows her own strength, and uses it to bring life to her household and her community. How many of us forget that the gifts we use to bring loveliness to our homes or the simple ways we serve our community are signs of our strength and dignity, worthy of praise? This woman is not one who has developed her creative gifts, her love of beauty, and her aptitudes simply to please herself. She radiates beauty to others and uses it at their service.

It is undeniable that each of us has something in common with this woman. We are all women of strength who bring beauty to this world in some way. Perhaps we can enter the sanctuary of this woman's home and gather a bit of inspiration rather than indignation at her creativity. Maybe there we can begin to dig away at whatever covers up our own bright, shiny jewel of giftedness and offer it to the world rather than hiding behind feelings of inadequacy, knowing that creativity and beauty are the genesis of true and lasting joy when they are given from a pure and humble heart.

~ NOURISHING OURSELVES WITH VIRTUE ~

In its great wisdom, our Church has given us the exact gift we need to know and understand the place between seeking sensual pleasure at the level of our passions and seeking true joy centered on the beauty of eternal things. It is the gift that allows us to trust our creative instincts and our longing for beauty We call that gift "virtue." In the Aristotelian sense, a virtue is expressed as the middle place between two extremes. Interestingly enough, rather than it being an extreme representation of our sanctity or pursuit of holiness, virtues are those characteristics we work to develop in ourselves because they anchor us squarely between the tug of our passions, the place of our emotions and desires, and the lowest level of our souls, and our intellect, the place where our faith is based on rational thinking. The anchor between those two places is truly the heart of our faith, the place where what we think and what we know and what our flesh longs for find a companionship with one another and a desire to please and obey our Father and Creator.

The virtues are the balance between who Eve was in Eden and who she was after the taste of the apple. They represent the place where we stand between complete naked innocence and sinful hiddenness from our Father. Virtue is that place where God covers us with his protection because we have placed ourselves where he can still reach us despite our sin and where we are cultivating our own garden that will bear good fruit. It is evidence of our spiritual green thumb inherited from Eden.

Just as the Proverbs 31 woman should not become a measuring

stick of all that we are not, neither should the practice of virtue leave us feeling the weight of constant failure. Seeing virtue as a middle ground allows us to embrace a spectrum where leaning at times toward one extreme or the other is not the equivalent of falling from a pedestal and then having it collapse upon us. Getting back to where we need to be does not require a total reconstruction effort, but a refocusing and shifting back to center where we experience the freedom of true joy.

For instance, when we speak of the virtue of love, the greatest of all the virtues, its spectrum is selfishness at one pole and enablement at the other. In order to become more loving, my effort is to recognize toward which pole I am most likely to lean and intentionally take steps toward my loving center place. I am a woman who without a doubt could use a bit more of the virtue of temperance in her life. Of the two poles on either side of temperance, licentiousness and strictness, I lean on the side of being too strict in my expectations of myself, of others, and of the world. Without despairing that I will never find my way to the perfection of temperance, I can instead simply begin to shift my leaning toward the middle ground step by step, surrendering my desire to control outcomes by heaping unrealistic expectations on myself and others, and knowing that each movement toward that center brings me to new levels of spiritual growth and wholeness.

Pursuing that kind of spiritual wholeness is reflected in our daily, bodily reality. It is noticeable in our conduct and produces a positive effect in our relationships. With every step toward intentional pursuit of living the virtues, we become more fully ourselves, both spiritually and bodily. As we do, we become more fully who God made us to be. In place of seeing the pursuit of virtue as a yoke of striving, we can see it as a walking backward toward the Eden reality, where we had no reason to fear God because we were as he designed us to be. Every movement toward the balance of virtue in our souls becomes an opportunity to stand more confidently bare before the Lord, knowing he will delight in seeing his image reflected more fully in us.

Being bare before the Lord in confidence frees us to pursue the gifts of creativity we have to offer, to uncover the precious gem we really are in the eyes of our Father, and reminds us who we were meant to be when he knitted us cell by cell in his own creative image. We can use those gifts to bring both ourselves and those around us a lasting beauty and joy that wafts the holy scent of Eden throughout our world.

~ Elise's Story ~

It was late 2013. My husband was a year and a half into treatment for aggressive cancer, recovering from a bone marrow transplant, a surreal four months of hospitalizations and round-the-clock caregiving that had required us to be three hours away from our six-, four-, and two-year-olds.

The stress was enough to shift things deep in my heart and soul and body: I started having strange dreams. I had a tremendously good therapist at the time. I sat in her office, describing a dream.

"I was undercover—a spy or secret agent of some sort," I said. "We were going into a fancy-dress party, and it was utterly important that no one knew who I was. But as we were going into the party, into danger, I buckled a wide leather strap around my throat. Someone said 'This will keep you safe.'"

My therapist waited, then said, "So, to be safe, you divide

your head from your heart. To protect yourself, you separate your mind from your body."

Defensiveness of a story I truly believed exploded in me. *Of course I do. Of course! And there is good reason for it! Our bodies and our feelings get us in trouble! Our minds wrestling with and killing our messy impulses and sensations are the only way we can do what God calls us to do!*

But I trusted this therapist and knew this misinformed belief had to be addressed, so one night in the bath, I tentatively followed her instructions, rubbing scented oil over each part of my body and saying thank you.

Thank you, legs, for carrying me for miles, giving me space and containment for my grief and despair. Thank you, hands, for flushing trilumen catheters and sanitizing the kitchen and turning around to rub a child's back or hold a baby close. Thank you, stomach, for healing after three C-sections, for stretching to hold my babies and then becoming part of me again, no matter how loosened you are. Thank you, breasts, for feeding three human beings.

A few years later, Chris had only months left to live. We were on our final and bittersweet beach vacation with his family. I was taking a short walk by myself on the beach, reflecting on life and pain and Mary's *fiat*, how God allowed the salvation of the world to depend on the free choice of a girl-child, how fully whole her response had to be: mental, emotional, and deeply embodied.

Suddenly, the wind came up and rushed along every pore of my skin, lifting my hair, intoxicatingly warm and cool together. I lifted my arms to it and felt embraced—knowing God's desire for each of us. Wind caressing water into waves; our whole bodies covered by these skins that are so exquisitely sensitive to touch and temperature and texture, light lavishly pouring through clouds and illuminating in stains of needless rose and gold and purple. The moment was Edenic, consuming; in it, I threw myself clumsily into God's arms, experiencing the joy of this holy sensuality created by the Lover of our lives.

~ Further Up and Further In ~

Have you ever considered the difference between temporal pleasures and lasting joy? What effect might this idea have on your behavior?

Did you have a preconceived notion of the Proverbs 31 woman before reading this chapter? Has anything changed after reading?

How well do you recognize your own creative gifts and the value of bringing beauty and joy to those around you? How might you go about digging deeper to uncover the gems of creativity that lie inside you undiscovered?

What are some of your strengths as a woman? How are you using them at the service of your household and community? What small act might you undertake to extend the reach of that strength?

———————— ⊗⊗⊗ ————————

CHAPTER SIX

EMBRACING VULNERABILITY

Sexuality and Self-Donation

For [Sarah] had been married to seven husbands, and the wicked demon Asmodeus had killed each of them before they had been with her as is customary for wives.

—TOBIT 3:8

Now when you are about to go to bed with her, both of you must first stand up and pray, imploring the Lord of heaven that mercy and safety may be granted to you. Do not be afraid, for she was set apart for you before the world was made. You will save her, and she will go with you.

—TOBIT 6:18

When the parents had gone out and shut the door of the room, Tobias got out of bed and said to Sarah, "Sister, get up, and let us pray and implore our Lord that he grant us mercy and safety." So she got up, and they began to pray and implore that they might be kept safe.

—TOBIT 8:4–5

• • • • •

As a Catholic teenager, I was deeply involved in youth groups and retreat programs, and I spent many nights listening to talks on purity, promising me great reward if I guarded my heart and body and only gave the gift of sexual intimacy away to the man I married. Unlike many of my peers, I actually took it all to heart. Not that I did not face temptation and get dangerously close to the edge more times than I care to admit, but on my wedding night, my metaphorical package was still wrapped and ready to offer to my husband.

The problem was that my young heart absorbed the message of purity to mean that having sex was bad and not having sex was good. As I entered marriage, I was swept into confusion about how to change that mindset because I had stood in church for an hour in a white dress. I was terrified of the vulnerability sexual intimacy would require of me, being inexperienced, and having felt the need to guard myself and my body from boys for all those years. I was ashamed of the ways I had failed during that time to guard myself fully and wondered if my new husband would somehow see the fingerprints of other men's hands in places they should not have been. I was a virgin, but not an untouched one.

Later, I would discover that past sexual abuse had affected my ability to be fully open to intimacy and experience the deeply satisfying physical and spiritual union we find described in St. John Paul II's "theology of the body." Christopher West in *Good News About Sex and Marriage* writes, "The most fulfilling sex possible comes when husband and wife unconditionally surrender themselves to each other—and receive each other—in a completely naked and honest revelation of their persons (which at an earlier point he describes as the indivisible union between body and soul)."[8]

In twenty years as a married couple, we have without a doubt discovered the physical mechanics of a mutually satisfying sexual relationship. But the concept of total self-donation on a physical and spiritual level as the goal of intercourse within marriage is a concept we are still reaching for. It has unique challenges for each of us; we inhabit bodies that both long for intimacy and bear the shame of sin—the falls of our own wills and the sins committed against us by others.

Whether we are married, single, or consecrated religious, we are working toward the same challenging goal, the complete surrender of our person, fully naked, whether bodily or spiritually, to another. Married women surrender themselves in that nakedness both physically and spiritually to their husbands. Single women surrender themselves to God in the nakedness of trusting his plan for their lives. Consecrated women surrender their souls to God in an intimacy that mirrors the marriage of man and woman, fully naked in the spiritual sense before their heavenly spouse.

For all of us, no matter our state in the life, the key to being able to move toward the vulnerability and risk that surrender requires is the virtue of chastity—a word that is often misunderstood and taken to mean abstinence from sexual intercourse, which is not chastity, but celibacy.

The *Catechism of the Catholic Church* describes chastity in this way: "Chastity means the successful integration of sexuality within the person and thus the inner unity of man in his bodily and spiritual being" (CCC, 2337). With this description in mind, we can consider cultivating chastity as a mandatory step toward our Eden identities. Chastity encompasses the integrity of person in which we were intended to live at creation, where there was no separation in our identity of our bodily and spiritual being. We existed in a harmony with ourselves that allowed us to live in full surrender to God. That same harmony with self is what enables the married woman to offer herself in an integrated spiritual and physical nakedness to her husband, accepting the invitation to complete self-donation in the marital embrace.

For almost every woman I know, there is a fear surrounding the risk that invitation requires of her. Whether it has its root in some sort of abuse or mistreatment by an individual or society as a whole, for most of us, our relationship with our bodies has been marred, which has created an unexpected and often undiscovered instinct to avoid complete vulnerability as a form of self-protection. Women, in particular, carry, along with their commitment to the virtue of chastity, burdens of shame that are often unaddressed in our relationships, in society, and even in the Church.

~ Considering Sexuality as Self-Donation ~

In any exposition of Catholic teaching on sexuality, and most directly in the Catechism of the Catholic Church, you will read that our sexuality is meant to bring us joy and pleasure, and this joy is derived from offering our sexuality as an act of self-donation either to the Lord, for those in an unmarried state, or to our spouse, for those in the married state.

With this as the basis of our viewpoint on sexuality, we can easily rebuff the notion that the Church views sexuality as something taboo or to be looked at with suspicion or even scorn. While promoting chastity as a virtue to be cultivated by all Christians, the Church calls the act of sexual intercourse among married couples "honorable and noble" insofar as that act "fosters self-giving and enriches the spouses in joy and gratitude" through the pleasure they derive from the act (CCC, 2362).

For single women, the gift of their chaste sexuality is cultivated in the bonds of friendship, imitating Christ's earthly relationships and fostering spiritual community in the world around us. Our sexuality is a gift in which we donate ourselves, body and soul, to spiritual communion with others. In no way does the Church suggest that our sexuality is to be seen as a malfunctioning of our souls or a purely physical desire that is base and disconnected from who God created us to be. Denying our sexuality as an integral part of our personhood diminishes our ability to form bonds of love with our neighbors, as we are all called by God to do.

God created us as sexual beings and does not ask us to deny that aspect of ourselves for any reason. Yet women still often struggle to embrace the Eden reality of their sexuality, the truth that our bodies were literally designed for sexual pleasure, with a complex system of nerves that form an organ whose only function is to heighten the chance of our reaching a satisfying sexual climax. God really wanted women to have pleasurable sexual experiences!

His will is, however, that we learn to master our sexuality through our intellect and will and not follow our passions into the disordered desires of lust. The woman who embraces her sexuality in a healthy union of body and soul and lives a life of self-donation as required by her state of life, is a woman who can live as Eve lived in Eden, naked and unashamed before God.

When we become ruled instead by our passions, and our sexuality is perverted from donative love to selfish pursuit, we relive Eve's sin, hiding ourselves from God and feeling our sexuality as something to be covered up and our nakedness as shameful. Thomas Merton remarked, "To be unknown to God is entirely too much privacy."[9] Particularly when it comes to our sexuality and its expression, when we separate the physicality of the gift from the spirituality of it, we seek a privacy from God, a place to hide from his sight, which is the antithesis of who he created us to be and how he created us to live.

The virtue of chastity, rooted in temperance (the ordering of our will and intellect to that of God, rather than being ruled by our passions) keeps us integrated body and soul in our sexuality, able to enjoy it as a gift, rather than fear it as a source of constant temptation. It is the heart of living a life of self-donation rather than the perversion of lust, a sexual selfishness that eventually leads to shame and self-preservation, to hiding from God, and living in fear that we have rendered ourselves unworthy of his love and mercy. In my experience, there is no aspect of our humanity more vulnerable to distortion by the world and its messages than our sexuality. And no sin can keep us bound up in doubt about the reality of God's mercy like sexual sin.

Whether we ever experience actual sexual abuse in our lives or not, all women are assaulted by the world regarding our sexual natures. On one side of the spectrum, we are sold the lie that we can separate our bodily good from our spiritual good and simply seek whatever brings us physical pleasure. On the other side, we are sold the lie that our bodies as they are, made in the image of our creator, are misshapen, put together all wrong, and that in altering them we can make them more beautiful and desirable. We are told in subtle and not so subtle ways that the rules of religion are oppressive to our sexual natures and that the pursuit of our own pleasure is what will bring us happiness. And in the church, there is a hush around women's sexuality outside of is procreative nature. We can talk about fertility and the quality of our mucus, but the mystery of true sexual pleasure for women and the things that prevent us from experiencing that are shrouded behind some sort of impenetrable veil it seems.

In regard to our sexuality and God's will for it, our culture repeats perpetually the question of the serpent, "Did God really say...?" We are assaulted by the messages of the world and are all too often connived into a sense of confusion about our sexuality that leads—similar to the way actual abuse does—to shame and self-loathing of our bodies and their sexual desires, and a view that our physicality must live at odds with our spirituality if we are to be serious about pursuing holiness.

But it is the world that has eaten the apple from the tree and distorted God's goodness. It holds that apple out to us and begs us to follow it into the disintegration of sin. It lies and tells us that what God really wants for us is pleasure and knowledge of who we really are, and that we can find that knowledge in our desires and passions rather than in obedience to God and his will for us.

Far too often, our bodies are the battleground on which the world wars for our spirits, and far too often, we have felt that the scars left from that battle destroy our ability to give and receive love intimately, whether from God, from others, or from ourselves. We hide ourselves away and pretend to find pleasure where we are really living in deep pain. We convince ourselves we are all alone in that pain, too far from the reach of God's mercy, and too wounded to seek true friendship and communion with others.

We are shamed for being too virgin-like if we pursue chastity with our whole hearts and shamed for being Jezebels if we fall into the trap, believe the lie, and pervert our true sexual nature into something God did not intend for us. From this place, how can we possibly freely give ourselves away to another, be it to our spouse in the sexual act or to God and others in celibate love?

One way to heal the damage that has been done to our view of ourselves and our sexuality as women is to walk the path back to Eden. We will find healing from abuse and assault, and freedom from the war the world has waged on our bodies and our sexuality, in remembering Eve, in embracing once again dependency on God, intimacy and consummate love with him, and shameless nakedness before him. These things come only through living under the protection of his holy will—the virtue of chastity and all that it entails for each of us. We will be able to embrace the vulnerability of self-donation in our human relationships only when we first embrace it in our relationship with our God and Creator.

~ In the Wedding Chamber with Sarah ~

Like an old epic film, the story of Sarah and Tobias, found in the book of Tobit, begins with two heart-wrenching scenes playing themselves out in two distinct places. First, the holy man Tobit cries out to God to grant him death because he has been blind for years and humiliated by having to have his wife provide for his family. He is burdened by the undeserved insults heaped on them by their community, and pleads with the Lord that he would rather die than live another day like this.

Far away in another town, young Sarah, the daughter of Raguel, stands in a chamber of her father's house praying a similar prayer. Sarah has borne yet again the insults of the servant maids of her father's house for her seven husbands who have been killed by a demon on their wedding night. Sarah is good and righteous and cannot bear another day of the torturous insults. She too, like Tobit, begs God to take her life, to remove her from this world and free her from her pain.

Tobit, knowing he has prayed for death and believing that God answers the prayers of his righteous ones, sets about preparing his young son Tobias to become the head of his family. He sends Tobias on a journey to bring back some money he has saved with a family member, with instructions to use it to bury him and to care well for his mother. Tobit offers his son his final fatherly counsel on how to be a man who lives well and honors God. He instructs Tobias to find a man to accompany him on the journey. The angel Raphael takes human form and becomes Tobias's travel companion, each step of the way maneuvering the circumstances according to the answer God has already spoken to the prayers of Tobit and Sarah that is yet to be revealed.

Tobias and Raphael are but a day into their journey when Raphael takes charge and reveals to Tobias that they will spend the night in the home of Raguel, Sarah's father, and that Tobias is to ask for Sarah as his wife. Tobias has heard the stories; he knows about the seven husbands who did not live through the first night with Sarah.

Raphael gives Tobias the simplest commands and the most concrete of promises. He is to think of the demon no more, to see Sarah in her loveliness and beauty, and to take her for his wife. He is to drive the demon away first through a ritual of cleansing, then join his new wife in prayer, and then, Raphael says, Sarah will be saved from the terror she has been living and be able to live a long life with him. Scripture tells us that from that moment, Tobias begins to love Sarah and be drawn to her (Tobit 6:16–17).

Tobias arrives at the home of Sarah's father and confidently asks for his right to marry her. Raguel reveals the lamentable truth of Sarah's past husbands, and encourages Tobias to give himself some time to consider what he is truly asking. But Tobias insists to her father that he desires no delay to think further about marrying Sarah.

We have seen nothing of Sarah since she pushed aside the thought of hanging herself and prayed instead for God to take her life. She stays hidden away upstairs, but Sarah must have some idea what is transpiring in her father's house at this moment. It is the eighth time a young man from her father's family line has arrived to eat and drink and "speak with him." Sarah cannot be ignorant to the significance of that conversation.

Have you ever prayed to God for something and then stood by watching nearly the opposite situation unfold? My heart beats hard for sweet Sarah here in this moment. It is such an intimate and difficult pain she bears, and here, the very same day she begs God to free her from it through death, it seems he is only throwing her right back into it.

When her mother enters her room bearing the news Sarah already knows, does Sarah feel a lump rise in her throat, are her tears hot with anger at God or the situation itself or her father who did not refuse this young man? Or are they turned inward on herself, in self-blame and a deep confusion about why she has been cursed by a God who claims that the righteous will prosper? What has Sarah's goodness, obedience, beauty, and loveliness gained her at this point but pain and shame?

Try to imagine the moments Sarah waits alone in that chamber for Tobias's arrival: the knot in her stomach, the pounding of her heart, the schizophrenic frenzy of conversation with God—"Why did you not hear my prayer?" "Did you hear it?" "Will it be different this time?" "What am I supposed to think, to do, to say to this poor man?" "What has he done to deserve this?" "What have I done to deserve this?" "Are you ever going to come save me from this pain, this horror?"

Everyone below is celebrating the wedding contract. Eating, drinking, reclining in ease. In heaven above, there is a great mercy flowing from the promises God has already made and answered for his beloved daughter Sarah. And yet alone in that room, Sarah waits in total vulnerability, complete emotional nakedness, the pain and sorrow of her past and all the lament she never deserved heavy in the air around her.

I wonder if Sarah paced in anxiety as she waited for the noise of the celebration to die down below her, chewing her lip and wringing her hands as she wiped hot tears away. I wonder if she climbed into that bed and rocked herself back and forth as I often do when panic tightens my throat and threatens to take my breath from me. Did she long for them to drink enough that they fell asleep and forgot all about the whole wedding night thing? Did she wish her mother would have just stayed, barred the door, and held her close, keeping her safe? When the door to that chamber opened and Tobias walked through it, how fast did Sarah's heart beat? Did she try to avert her eyes from the young man whose death she was certain would come, not wanting to see the confidence, the goodness, the loveliness that surely graced his features?

As Sarah awaits the repeating story line of her life, the pain and the horror she has known too many times, Tobias stands firmly in obedience to answer to God's commands. When he places the elements of his oddly prescribed ritual and lights the match of offering, can it be felt in the room, the fleeing of Asmodeus, who has caused so much devastation?

Has Sarah learned to sense him? Had she trembled all those other nights when she knew he was near, or held her eyes shut tight hoping she could wish or pray him away? Did her body tighten in fear? Did she know as soon as he was gone that it was done? Did she look fully upon Tobias for the first time in recognition of the miracle of her freedom?

What beautiful symbolism there is in that moment when Tobias takes Sarah's hand and raises her to her feet, lifts her from her bed of shame, and takes her naked and vulnerable before God, to pray. He invokes the example of Eve's creation for Adam and pleads to God for mercy for himself and his sweet Sarah, confident that his chaste love, his obedience, will bring them freedom: "I now am taking this kinswoman of mine, not because of lust, but with sincerity. Grant that she and I may find mercy and that we may grow old together" (Tobit 8:7).

As they pray, the very people who moments earlier had celebrated confidently with Tobias while Sarah waited in anguish upstairs are now outside digging his grave, lamenting his naive confidence that all would be well. Meanwhile in Egypt, Raphael is binding the demon Asmodeus and dealing him his final blow. And in that wedding chamber, a union is being consummated, its very own celebration. Tobias has won God's heart with his obedience and routed the demon that plagued Sarah. Sarah's vulnerable nakedness is finally and for the first time a source of pleasure and love rather than horror, pain, and shame. The contrast of the scenes is striking.

The story nears its end with the curious family sending someone to take a peek into that chamber, to look for the body they must bury, and to console Sarah in her renewed anguish. So imagine for one moment the shock and then delight that flooded Raguel's home that night when the door creaked open and, in the flickering candlelight, the sleeping forms of Sarah and Tobias were revealed, lying in a peaceful embrace.

We do not know how Sarah lived out the rest of her days with Tobias, but we do know that she was received into his home, into his family, into his community with love and joy and celebration. We do know that the shame and pain she once felt in her nakedness before was replaced with a marital love that brought no shame or pain to her in her vulnerability, but instead great joy. And while the Scriptures do not name it as such, every one of us who have known that pain, along with Sarah, can call that a miraculous healing.

~ Embracing Vulnerability ~

In the story of Tobias and Sarah, much detail and attention is paid to how Tobias is able to defeat the demon Asmodeus by overcoming his fear, following the counsel and commands of Raphael obediently, and loving Sarah with a chaste love. Little detail is given to us of what actually occurs in Sarah's mind and heart other than her painful prayer begging for her own death and the hot tears she cries when faced with yet another possibility to experience the pain that has broken her.

In much the same way, the work produced by the Church on human sexuality in more recent years based on the "theology of the body" tends to focus heavily on two aspects: the duty of men to overcome their temptations toward selfishness, lust, and fornication in order to embrace the self-donative love that is truly life-giving in marriage, and the couple's responsibility to respect the procreative aspect of sexual love in accordance with the church's teachings so that their relations may be life-giving in the truest sense.

There is an unspoken assumption that the role of the married woman is to offer her body as a receptacle of the self-donative love of her husband, to embrace sex as a gift of self, and as long as they can come to terms with making that gift complete by avoiding artificial contraception, all should be well, especially if that intimacy results in conception.

Yet when women begin to tell their stories, and we take a hard look at statistics, the reality is that few women can embrace their sexuality free from the effects of some kind of abuse.[10] If we additionally consider survivors of childhood sexual abuse, women who have been emotionally or verbally abused or assaulted, raised in families affected by alcohol, or experienced codependency or emotional neglect, the stark truth is that few women enter adulthood without scars marking their experience of sexuality and intimacy in relationships.

We live in a world full of noise about women and what it means to be sexy and desirable, most of it promoting a standard we inherently reject as ridiculous but still carry around inside us as an accusation of inadequacy. We are left wondering if we can believe that God really looked at our naked feminine bodies and called them good. Within our Church culture, in earnest but misguided attempts to encourage us to pursue chastity and purity in our youth, many of us experience a reverse indoctrination that our bodies are bad and are to be mistrusted.

The result is a hush over an all-too-pervasive reality about human sexuality in the Church: Women often carry a debilitating shame and fear of the vulnerability and intimacy required for a truly healthy sexual relationship. While many men must overcome a sexual selfishness the world has implanted in their hearts in order to learn to give themselves in self-donative love to their wives, many wives struggle to see themselves as a gift worthy of giving to their husbands rather than a shameful and unacceptable imitation of what a woman should truly be.

Where do we go then, as women, to heal, to recognize our wounds and hurts, to express them in safety, and to find our way to wholeness? First, we need to find one another. We need to know we are not alone in the difficulties we face when it comes to intimacy and vulnerability. The only way we can know that is to know other women experience it too. We have far too often silenced the conversation for fear of being salacious or scandalous. I mean, holy women do not sit around talking about sex unless they are at marriage prep or natural family planning classes, right? Until they do. Because we must. Without the safety of other women walking this path with us to relieve us of the fear that we are utterly alone in our fears, pain, and even wild enjoyment of our own sexuality, shame can root itself so deeply inside us that the sexual intimacy God intended for our joy becomes a yoke that is heavy and a burden that is anything but light.

We need honest women who earnestly endeavor to do God's will to lead one another to his consummate and compassionate love. There is no doubt we need a counter-balance to the idea of sexual freedom and liberation, of the safety of following our passions, that the world, even the wider Christian world, holds out to us. We can be that balancing weight for one another. In the assurance that we are not alone, we can also remind one another that God does in fact desire that we experience the inherent goodness of our sexuality and the higher pleasure that comes from experiencing marital sex in the freedom of total self-donation.

Many of the women earnestly trying to live the deep vulnerability the Church rightly asks of us in marital intimacy are secretly wondering what is wrong with us that we can't seem to get it right and find it as pleasurable as it should be, yoking ourselves with shame and insecurity based in wounds buried so deeply we do not even remember where they came from. Another large percentage of us know exactly where our shame comes from; we are blocked from the fulfillment of true self-donative love by our inability to fully receive God's mercy and forgive ourselves for our own past sexual sin or to find a path to healing from past abuse.

If we are to find a way to heal those wounds and truly be able to embrace the vulnerability required to stand fully naked, physically and emotionally, before our husbands and know sexual love without shame, we must recognize them and have the courage to seek help and mercy, to find a way to know ourselves as the unblemished gift that we are and not as part gift and part ugliness we must hide away and make sure is never discovered.

This is where cultivating our Eden instinct in so many other aspects of life becomes vital. If we can begin to find our way back to Eve in the way we live our lives in virtue and creativity, in the way we practice self-care, in the way we seek mercy and grace in the Church, then the path is laid for us to rely on one another for support and to lead one another back to the healing hand of God. We need to make our way back to our actual physical nakedness in order to see sexual vulnerability with new eyes, eyes that relish our ability to give ourselves completely and to experience the ecstasy of the marital embrace with new confidence, because we know that we were created as gift for the joy of that intimacy. Grace and mercy can bring us back to that awareness.

Chastity is the path that keeps us walking toward a healthy sexuality. But when all is said and done, few women enter into the sexual intimacy of marriage without some scar on their souls that makes the intimate marital chastity of total self-donation perilous and painful for them. We need a path that leads us out of that confusion, back to the places we need to be held by God, healed of our wounds, offered mercy, and given permission to accept it. It is a path from the sexual chaos of today's world back to the simplicity of the Eden life, where vulnerability was how we were made and expected to live, not a weakness to fear, and there was no shame to cloud nakedness in confusion and pain. A path that allows us to then offer it as gift to our spouses, because we have learned first to see it as gift in ourselves.

There is no doubt that God designed humans to experience joy and pleasure in sexual intimacy. There is no doubt he desires it for his daughters. There is grace abundant for us to erase any doubt *we* may have, and open our hearts to see the gifts we truly are and offer them freely and without reserve to the men we love. This is our loving God's will for us, and we can embrace it by embracing one another and walking together toward true sexual freedom in Christ, freedom from all shame, freedom that embraces the beauty of sexual intimacy given as a gift to our beloved from our beloved. And if the men who love us are also heeding that call, well then, we can only expect that one day, beyond the mechanical physical pleasure of sex, we will find a new level of satisfaction, as our embrace becomes, as it was meant to be, a reflection of God's total giving of himself to us in consummate love.

Judy's Story

With my body I thee worship.... In the name of the Father, and of the Son, and of the Holy Ghost.

—Wedding Vows, *Anglican Book of Common Prayer*

Present your bodies as a living sacrifice, holy and acceptable to God, your spiritual worship.

—Romans 12:1

My idea of physical intimacy in a second marriage was to close the curtains, turn off the lights, and keep my eyes shut tight. After all, I had a million reasons to hide. I was a fifty-two-year-old widow with a soft belly, varicose veins, and stretch-marked breasts—the crowns of the five children I had lovingly borne and nursed. The thought of unveiling my body for Mark made me lightly cringe, and I figured that sparing him that sight might actually be a mercy.

My precious new husband, however, who had never before been married or with a woman, had a different idea. I will never forget the first few times we made love and how I, being the one with experience, gingerly instructed him that people keep their eyes closed while having sex.

"Why would they want to do that?" he asked with genuine surprise. "I want to look into your eyes and contemplate your beautiful body. It seems to me that's a large part of the enjoyment of sex."

Crap, I thought. *This is not going to be easy.*

My body has always been a source of deep shame for me, owing to sexual abuse in childhood, seven brothers under whose glare I was constantly pronounced "fat" (even though I was thin as a rail at the time), and a lifetime of wounded relationships with men that fueled the belief that my body is flawed and needs improvement. Truth be told, I've never been comfortable in a bathing suit on my best day, and there hasn't been a day in my life since entering puberty when I haven't been trying to lose weight.

"You want to contemplate my beauty?" I asked, laughing so heartily at the suggestion that tears literally rolled down my face. But overcorrecting with humor could not hide my fear of self-exposure.

Wanting no part of keeping the lights on, I agreed to candles only, figuring their subdued flames would at least keep my body shrouded in shadows. But over time, as I began to trust Mark's love for me and deeper intimacy grew between us, gazing into his eyes during the marital embrace—and letting him see me—began to bring enthralling joy and pleasure. Instead of an occasion of hiding, I started to experience sexual intimacy as in-to-me-see, and baring my body before my beloved as an expression of the soul baring that was taking place both in and out of the bedroom whenever Mark and I were together.

I was even heard to exclaim a few times while looking in the mirror: "Damn, I look good!"

Love heals us that way.

Interestingly, the word *vulnerable* comes from the Latin word *vulnerare*, which means to wound, hurt, or injure. How many of us blanche at vulnerability precisely because we have been wounded in untold ways by flaming arrows that left us burning and exposed? But vulnerability also implies openness, receptivity, and surrender: the very qualities that make it possible for two to become one flesh, and for that intimate God-conceived union to become an earthly conduit of heaven's foretaste.

~ FURTHER UP AND FURTHER IN ~

What has your personal definition of chastity been up until now? Has anything you read in the chapter broadened or changed that definition?

If you have never read the book of Tobit in the Bible, try to find the time to do so. Reflect on the epic nature of the story from the earliest moments of Tobit's and Sarah's separate prayers to the journey that joins the two to the end result. What can this story teach you about God, your own vulnerability before him, and his faithfulness to our prayers?

Do you find vulnerability and intimacy in the physical or emotional sense difficult? Have you examined what wounds in your life might lead to that difficulty? Have you sought counsel for the healing of those wounds? If you have not, consider seeking professional, spiritual, and/or psychological help. Pray for the courage to allow yourself to heal.

Do you have intimate relationships with female friends with whom you can honestly share your stories? Have you avoided the topic of sexuality with these trusted friends? Consider if there might be an appropriate way to engage this topic and allow the women in your life to tell their stories and come out of the shame of hiding in knowing they are not alone.

CHAPTER SEVEN

FAITHFULNESS IN THE FLESH

Suffering and Surrender

Her rival used to provoke her severely, to irritate her, because the Lord had closed her womb. So it went on year by year; as often as she went up to the house of the Lord, she used to provoke her. Therefore Hannah wept and would not eat.

—1 SAMUEL 1:6–7

But Hannah answered, "No, my lord, I am a woman deeply troubled; I have drunk neither wine nor strong drink, but I have been pouring out my soul before the Lord. Do not regard your servant as a worthless woman, for I have been speaking out of my great anxiety and vexation all this time."

—1 SAMUEL 1:15–16

"For this child I prayed; and the Lord has granted me the petition that I made to him. Therefore I have lent him to the Lord; as long as he lives, he is given to the Lord."
She left him there for the Lord.

—1 SAMUEL 1:27–28

· · · · ·

The day I buried my son, a baby boy but three months old who had died in his sleep—the sixth boy born to my husband and me—was without a doubt the most difficult day of my life thus far. And yet, I had developed a plan to celebrate the moment. After the prayers of burial were prayed, we followed his tiny coffin to its final resting place, weeping in our pain and watching the men slide it inside, close the space, and place the heavy marble back over it, marking the finality of my little Bryce's earthly life. Then I turned to our family and friends, and through tears explained that while we would never celebrate the birthdays we had imagined as we awaited and then held this tiny little boy in our arms, today, even as we grieved so greatly his loss, we would celebrate his glorious entry into heaven. A friend who had helped me prepare my plan walked forward with a great rainbow bouquet of helium balloons and handed one to everyone in attendance. I began, and together, we all sang "Happy Birthday" to my son, who had been born into the Lord's heavenly presence. Then we released those balloons and watched them float away into the bright blue September sky, a sign of joy, an offering of my little one to the Lord, even as my heart broke with grief. There is a photo of that moment that a dear friend snapped of my youngest son, barely two years old, clasping the string of his balloon with two chubby hands at the ready to release it, with a wide smile of excitement stretched across his face. It is engraved in my mind forever as an example of what it means to trust God with a childlike faith. While I do not think for one moment that God begrudged my broken, lamenting heart, I do think he longed for me to know that the joy on my sweet boy's face was an equally true response to our suffering, not a childlike ignorance, but a childlike innocence that trusted completely that he could grab that moment of celebration amid suffering and live it fully, appreciate it, and let it go along with his red balloon.

When we move from the glory of the creation story, through the pain of the fall, and into the epic tale of redemption, the question that remains for us at the end of it all is the question of suffering. What are we to do with ourselves when this world outside of Eden breaks our hearts, takes from us the things we most love, or denies us the things we most long for? What are we to do when our bodies fail us or the physical world assaults with pain? When the suffering of our earthly existence becomes a spiritual crisis, a question we cannot seem to ever wrestle a full peace from, no matter how much we plead with our God, how are we supposed to go on?

There are countless examples of women in the Bible who suffered great losses, great pain, and sought God for answers and relief. In the lineage of women from my own family, there is a grandmother who buried two sons and two husbands before succumbing to cancer. My own mother has buried a husband and a son. A sister buried a baby boy born too early. The loss of my own son was followed by four miscarriages. And then there are the stories of friends and acquaintances: young mothers battling breast cancer then leaving five small children behind, infertility and unfaithfulness in marriage, abuse, rape, failed adoptions, children who grow up to be addicts, suffer from mental illness, commit suicide.

Yet again and again, I watch women take their pain, get up, keep going, and somehow, through all their wrestling and questioning and the deep doubt that God can be who he says he is, trust him enough to still have hope, not only for heaven, but for their lives this side of heaven. Our Eden lives destroyed, and suffering and death we were never meant to know always at our door, still our incarnate beings find their way back to hope amid suffering. Still we find a way to look at the body and blood of our Redeemer, our God made man, who suffers with and for us, and believe that there is value to our pain. Still we make our way through our brokenness to a sense of wholeness that only comes with the holy offering of ourselves to God and trust in his mercy even in our darkest days.

~ Considering Suffering ~

There is not a single human being who has lived to the age of awareness who would not admit that suffering is an inevitable part of our earthly lives. And yet, for the Christian believer, there is a significance to the question of suffering and its meaning that goes beyond its mere inevitability. We know suffering and death did not exist in Eden and entered the world through the fall. We know we are promised they will be no more in heaven. And yet, here we are on earth, facing them daily. But if we are believers in the incarnation of our God in the body of his Son, who lived and breathed as a man here on earth, and we profess that the possibility for our redemption from sin and hope of eternal life lie in his crucifixion, death, and resurrection, then we must embrace the reality that suffering can have a redemptive nature for us as incarnated beings as well.

I do not think there is a more universal spiritual dilemma among Christians than how we are supposed to deal with suffering: how to explain it, how to find meaning in it, how to understand what God intends for us in it, and how to do it well. Death and suffering are the great mysteries of our faith that plague us with questions and doubts more often than any other mystery of God. Many misunderstandings about suffering underlie our confusions.

We hear that God does not cause or intend our suffering, and yet we read quote after quote by the saints of the Church pleading with God to delay their deaths to prolong their suffering for him. While we could attribute that to a time and place where suffering was understood differently than it is today, I could also quote you any number of recently written Christian articles and blog posts that make subtle and not so subtle claims that God causes our suffering so he can purify us and make us holy.

One thing is certain, nothing on earth makes it apparent that we live a connected physical and spiritual existence so much as the realities of suffering and death. Yet we are mistaken to believe that God desires us to seek suffering so we can achieve holiness. In their ideal condition at creation, God endowed man and woman with immunity from suffering and death. Their choice to turn their backs on the love he offered them in Eden brought sin and death into the world.

God could have chosen in justice to leave humanity to suffer and die with no future hope. Or he could have chosen simply to offer mercy to humanity and reparation for sin through no tangible action, a hidden spiritual shift that returned humanity to its Eden state. But the God who loves us freely desires that we, in return, love him freely. To open a path back to Eden to us in our sinful natures, he chose to send his Son to share our human form and suffer the justice required by our sin to restore us to the hope of once again living eternally in our original state with him.

By imbuing the inevitable suffering and death we will face as humans with a redemptive quality, God offers us new hope—that in joining our suffering to his we can create the communion of relational love with him that our Eden instincts long for, and that we can bring about some good in this fallen world by living in his image and likeness, including embracing the crosses we encounter in our lives.

Our all-loving God does not desire that we seek suffering to become holy, but he does desire that we surrender to him in our suffering so that in our brokenness, his mercy can make us whole again. In being broken open by suffering, we are offered the opportunity to let those open spaces be filled with the mercy and compassion of our God, and in the depth of that mercy to be moved to love him more deeply. Surrendering to suffering is the path we walk backwards through the pain of the fall toward the life of Eden.

As women, we are deeply affected in the aspects of our God-given feminine natures—the relational, creational, and incarnational aspects of our being—by the suffering that we encounter in this life. There is no denying that our bodies bear this pain in a uniquely feminine way, from the myriad of pains surrounding our procreational possibilities, to the physical and emotional pain our bodies can cause us, to the brokenness that comes from and pours into our relationships. Women's suffering is, in fact, uniquely feminine. And our ability to see the cracks and scars it leaves us as a part of our unique loveliness that draws us into deeper communion with our God is often obscured by the pain of seeing ourselves as failures either because of the fact that we are suffering or because we believe we are suffering badly or wrongly—that we are not becoming holy enough in our pain.

Recently, as I confronted an intense period of emotional pain in my life, I sat questioning God about my suffering. "I am drowning," I cried out, "And where are you? Why are you not coming to rescue me? All I hear are the voices of all these experts who stand safely on their docks and yell advice at me as to how to save myself. Who is going to get in the water with me and drag me to safety if not you?" If you remember from an earlier chapter, drowning is a particularly anxiety-provoking memory for me, so it was with a truly anguished heart that I pleaded this prayer to the Father. I sat, feeling my quickened breath, waiting for an answer that would relieve me of this burden of pain that felt insurmountable. And quietly, simply, God's voice came with the answer, "But, my love, what if I am the sea?"

I have spent long months thinking on the meaning of this answer, in which God offered me the opportunity to see all that I was struggling against—my pain, my childhood wounds, my losses, the deaths that have scarred my life, my relational woes—as an opportunity to stop fighting to keep to my head above the waters I saw as so threatening and instead let go, still myself, and trust that he would hold me up, floating just above the surface, able to breathe freely.

Some of us find ourselves in the choppy waters of the ocean because we have jumped in headfirst through sin. Others find ourselves tossed from a boat on which we thought we were charting a course straight through God's will. For many of us, life has thrown us a combination of circumstances that leave us unable to distinguish exactly how the drops of water became a sea big enough to swallow us up in our suffering and pain.

Yet for all of us, especially for us women who can have such difficulty in seeing our suffering as worthwhile to God, this image of being held by the very waters we are afraid to drown in is such a powerful metaphor of God's mercy and what he wants us to do with our suffering. We do not have to know how the ocean filled, nor become expert swimmers to escape its threat, nor flail ourselves into weariness hoping to be noticed and saved. All we have to do is lie back in that water and surrender to God's unending mercy and compassion, trusting that no matter how heavy, how sinful, how sorrowful, how doubt-riddled, how angry we are, he can hold it all. He can keep us from drowning in it. He can keep us breathing.

The kind of suffering that makes us holy, that allows us to become participants in the redemptive love of Christ, is not a perfection of *how* we suffer, nor an acceptance of *why* we suffer, but a surrender to the love of Father, an offering of our brokenness and pain as love back to the God who offered his brokenness and pain as love for us.

As women, we have unique pains based on the way we bear the image of God in our feminine form. Imagine then, the great delight it is to him when, in place of trying to forge that pain into something worthwhile to offer him, we simply offer our whole selves to him, pain and all, and trust that his love will cover us and hold us and keep us breathing until we can make our way back to Eden, to the eternal paradise where he awaits us with the same longing we await a life without pain, suffering or death.

~ IN THE TEMPLE WITH HANNAH ~

In Scripture, the most repeated experience of pain for a woman is to be barren, or unable to bear children, and the most joyful evidence of God's faithfulness is when that woman is finally gifted with a child. It is repeated so often we can begin to see it as a metaphor for whatever pain and loss we as women face, and whatever way the Lord brings life to our barren places and generates fruitfulness in our lives.

Hannah, a key figure in the first book of Samuel, is a woman who is bearing the deep suffering of being unable to bear a child. She has suffered so long and her pain has become so deep that she is unable even to verbally express it when asked by her husband the cause for her sadness. She has no more words. She can no longer eat or drink, her pain so all-encompassing that even the thought of meeting her most basic need for nourishment requires too much from her.

If you have ever experienced depression or know someone who has, these symptoms will feel eerily familiar to you. Curling into oneself, unable to express the depth of one's pain and one's sadness, and giving up on communication is a telltale sign of depression, as is an inability to remember how to complete the most basic of daily tasks. If you have been in that place or can easily imagine yourself having fallen that far into some pain you have borne in your life, then you can feel the heaviness that seeps from Hannah's heart throughout her entire body, making her leaden with the weight of her pain, and unable to care about much else.

Scripture reveals a very real, vulnerable picture of womanhood in Hannah, who seems to respond the way so many of us women do to her suffering. When she can enter the temple and stand before God, she pours her anguished heart out to him, quietly trying to hide her pain from the sight of others, her broken heart spilling over to God in a deluge that she has held inside for so long. The priest Eli, watching the contortion of her pained lips and the rapidity of the words that she pours out, assumes that Hannah must be drunk and confronts her.

Can you imagine the shame heaped upon Hannah in her pain when her private conversation with God not only calls the attention of the priest to her, but convinces him she must have come to the temple drunk? I know all too well how it feels to be nearly drunk on pain, confused, your thoughts an incoherent fog, your body betraying your private broken heart with its trembling hands and quivering lips. I have been the woman stared at in church as my pain spilled uncontrollably out, and I have known the embarrassment Hannah must have felt as Eli approached her with this accusation.

But Hannah, even in her suffering, is so willing to wait on God to fulfill her broken heart's desire that, after explaining herself to Eli, she promises the now-convinced priest that should she be granted a son, she will give him as a gift to the temple to be trained up as a priest from the earliest of ages, as soon as she has weaned him from the breast. While in those times that may have meant Hannah had a full five years with this son for whom her heart has broken and broken again, it is still a sacrifice too great for most of us to even consider.

When Hannah is indeed given the gift of a little boy whom she names Samuel, she stays true to her promise, and upon his being weaned from her breast, she delivers him to Eli at the temple, leaving him in the care of the old priest. I know the small grief it was for me when each of my babies weaned, the moment I suddenly realized it had been days since they had demanded to be nursed and the sweet intimacy of that relationship was over. I also know the pain of having lost my sweet little baby Bryce after praying all through my pregnancy for a long and healthy nursing relationship with him. I cannot imagine how Hannah found the strength to give up the joy she had found in finally having a son and turn him over to God and his priest voluntarily, in gratitude for God's faithfulness to her after such prolonged suffering.

Scripture tells us with certainty that when Hannah delivered Samuel to the temple, he was still very young, and yet she seems happy to "have lent him to the Lord" and have "left him there for the Lord." Like Abraham, who willingly gave Isaac to God until God returned him, Hannah makes a sacrifice of the hope for which she has most suffered.

Do you think Hannah left Samuel in Eli's hands and never looked back? Never longed to have her little boy with her in her home again? Never teared up with longing to feel the softness of his hair on her lips, take in his scent, or feel the weight of his head against her chest? Surely the cracks left in Hannah's heart that had suffered so much seeped with a new kind of pain and longing. But as a witness to God's faithfulness, that pain was laced with a new kind of hope, a redemptive hope. Hannah's ability to give Samuel back to God as a gift is a witness to the fact that all her suffering had brought her to a deep trust in God's goodness, one that gave her the confidence to release to him even the very gift she had begged for.

Hannah's suffering had opened her wide before God, broken her through and revealed her fully, in all her vulnerability and pain to him. She learned to accept that even as her body delayed in delivering her deepest longing, God was there to sustain her very next breath, every uttered prayer that left her lips drawing him to her in his great compassion and tender-hearted mercy.

And so it was that after making an offering to God of her son and leaving him to grow up in the temple under Eli's care and tutelage, she could long for her sweet Samuel and yet trust God to be faithful in her suffering. So deeply surrendered was she to God's love that she could enter the temple once a year with a new hand-sewn robe in which to clothe the child of her deepest longings and leave him once again in the heart of God, the heart she had learned to trust even as her own broke.

~ Becoming Holy in Wholeness ~

In the introduction of this book, I proposed the thought that we cannot be spiritually well without integrating the incarnational, or embodied, aspects of our human experience with our souls. In short, we cannot disconnect ourselves from our bodies as something other than the spiritual aspect of our humanity. In fact, this concept is the root of many heresies in the history of the Catholic Church.

When we consider womanhood and suffering in light of that truth, we are likely to react with fierce emotions. Because the reality of being a woman is that our bodies are often a source of suffering, or at the very least doubt and confusion for us. The normal changes of puberty, pregnancy, postpartum, and menopause can run emotional shock waves that register as trauma through many women's relationship with God and themselves. Then there is the high risk that Catholic women who live the call to embrace our procreative potential will experience the pain and loss of miscarriage, infertility, and other hormone-related problems at higher rates than other women and with higher emotional costs.

Above and beyond these more common experiences of pain are women who are suffering disabling illnesses or are struck by cancer or other serious diseases. And then there is the daily battle for our bodies against abuse, assault, and general disrespect for women in our society. Often too, we encounter those in our own church who feel it their duty to question our morality if they judge our family to be too small, our children to be poorly behaved, or the life we have chosen to live somehow unbecoming to our femininity.

If we hold to the truth that suffering is an inevitable part of the human experience, we can as assuredly claim that the experience of physical suffering or emotional pain related to our female makeup is also inevitable in our lifetimes.

So how can these suffering bodies or the emotional pain our physical reality brings us do anything to make us spiritually well?

Victor Frankl in *Man's Search for Meaning* recounts his experiences as a psychologist in the concentration camps of World War II, and uses them to illustrate his main conclusion, that a human being can survive even the worst suffering if meaning can be found in it. He writes,

> For the first time in my life I saw the truth as it is set into song by so many poets, proclaimed as the final wisdom by so many thinkers. The truth—that Love is the ultimate and highest goal to which man can aspire. Then I grasped the meaning of the greatest secret that human poetry and human thought and belief have to impart: The salvation of man is through love and in love.[11]

If love is the ultimate goal to which we aspire, and our salvation comes in and through love, then we have a response to the mystery of suffering that gives us hope. We can find meaning in our bodily suffering and emotional pain by allowing it to draw out our need to be loved. We need to learn to love ourselves, including our incarnated, physical selves, we need to learn to let others love us in our pain and brokenness, and we need to let the desperation of our suffering draw us into deeper love with our God as we find ourselves more dependent on him.

In recent years, it has been popular to replace the word "suffering" with "brokenness" in inspirational Christian writing. There is a push to accept our brokenness as a gift. And yet, I fear we may be imbibing the message that the brokenness itself is the good we desire, that the level of our brokenness is in some way equivalent to the level of our holiness. The truth is, no suffering endured or embraced for the sake of the suffering itself brings us to holiness.

It is in allowing the suffering that inevitably comes to us to make us needy for God's mercy and desperate for his love that we find holiness. For God's love fills our broken places and is redemptive to our souls even when he does not heal us physically. This is how we are made whole, or spiritually well, in relationship to our embodied brokenness—when we can accept it as love given and received by God.

It is in that wholeness that we achieve a higher level of holiness. As we reflect more truly the image of God imprinted on us, body and soul, by accepting even the imprint of our suffering Savior, we become more like God, and we learn to depend more deeply on his love to sustain us. If we allow our suffering and brokenness to bring us back toward Eden dependence and Eve's total vulnerability before God, we are becoming both more whole and more holy.

Suffering and pain, especially our uniquely female experiences of it, can be a source of shame for us. And it becomes even more so when our bodies defy us by telling our secrets to the world. When emotional pain becomes emotional eating and our weight fluctuates, shame heaps upon shame. When infertility or miscarriage breaks our hearts and then we are asked if we are pregnant, or when we're going to have the next one, and tears uncontrollably brim to the surface, the shame can be more debilitating than the pain. When something as simple as acne returning to us well into our adult years because of the hormone shifts of menopause triggers the trauma of our puberty and the confusing rapidity with which our bodies became unknown to us, we can be surprised by unexpected shame.

This shame can threaten to disconnect our bodily reality from our spiritual state. If we have been seeking intimacy with God for any amount of time, and building a relationship where we are learning to trust his love for us, suddenly finding ourselves cloaked in shame on a physical level can eat away at that intimacy without our even realizing it. Our hiding from God does not come all at once like Eve's, but gradually, as the idea that our bodies and the pain they cause us is unacceptable seeps into our souls and compels us to hide it, seeking safety in being unseen.

For this reason, finding meaning in our uniquely feminine physical experience and its varied sufferings and pains is imperative to our pursuit of holiness. The wholeness with which we come before God is the extent to which we embrace the nakedness that brings us our salvation in and through love, as Frankl describes. As we reveal ourselves and our pain fully to God, on both an emotional and spiritual level, we stand naked and vulnerable before him and confess our need to be loved. Since we are created by a God who is love and therefore can only respond in love, we find our pain bringing us into deeper intimacy with him. That growing intimacy draws love from us that we long to return to God for the great mercy he has shown us. It also allows us to learn to have mercy on ourselves and accept the unchangeable defects or illnesses of our bodies and minds and treat ourselves with kindness and compassion.

This is a process of growing toward wholeness as a person. It is the same process that brings growth in holiness. We can, therefore, free ourselves from the notion that holiness is a competition to see who can be more broken and embrace the truth that our holiness lies not in how much or how well we suffer, but in our wholeness, in drawing meaning from our inevitable suffering that brings us deeper into the fullness of love, where we are embraced by our suffering savior and made spiritually well by his compassionate mercy.

~ Kim's Story ~

I am not a mistake. My body is not a mistake.

Sure, I have Charcot-Marie Tooth Disease (CMT), scoliosis, arthritis, sleep apnea, chronic dry eyes, and even annoying adult acne. But this clumsy body was fearfully and wonderfully made by our one true God.

Don't get me wrong. I'm not always so chipper about my situation. When I want to take a road trip to visit a friend but can't due to my horrible reflexes and lack of a driver's license, I get frustrated. When I need to stop a simple activity like laundry because of pain in my hip, I get frustrated that I am not like the great saints who bore their crosses with such grace and patience. Many days, I don't want to take up my cross.

But I realize that attitude will get me nowhere. I learned that at an early age. I have always had a disability requiring some level of adaptation at home and school. Even so, my parents placed high expectations on me, as they did on my siblings. With those expectations, I was able to go on to college, earn a degree, and begin an independent life. I had to conquer many barriers along the way. My grandmother purchased a motorized scooter wheelchair for my high school graduation so I could get around my college campus. To this day, I still use a similar wheelchair to scoot around town during warmer seasons. I can choose isolation, or I can choose to interact with the world around me. I choose the latter!

I will admit, for many years my biggest insecurity was whether or not I would ever find a man who would look beyond my disability. This may sound funny, but being an inspiring person doesn't often translate well in the dating scene.

The good news is that because I was made in the likeness and image of God, I was, indeed, created for love! I met a wonderful man named Bruce while attending a retreat many years ago. We have now been married for twenty-three years. We knew that we were called to love not only each other, but whatever children God would send our way. God blessed us with one biological son who was stillborn, Gabriel, and forty-one foster children over the years.

When Bruce and I were first married, I was physically stronger and able to work full-time. Now, he has to assist me with many basic daily tasks. As my physical health has deteriorated, God has spoken to my heart in new ways. I have more time to focus on praying for my amazing husband and our family and friends. My love for the Catholic Church has matured, which has pushed me into the joyful life of evangelization. My disability is an undeniable part of my life, but it does not define me. In John's Gospel, Jesus tells us a man's blindness from birth was not due to his parents' sin, but so that the glory of God may be shown through him.

That is my hope...to always show and speak of the glory of God!

~ FURTHER UP AND FURTHER IN ~

Have you ever felt confused by the suffering you've experienced? Wondered why God would allow it or even felt that he caused it? How did you work through your confusion?

Consider Hannah's reaction to her suffering and then God's answer to her prayers? Would this have been your response? What can we learn from Hannah?

Do you think that the physical reality of living in a female body brings us uniquely feminine experiences of shame and pain? Are there particular areas in your life where this is true?

How can you let your physical suffering bring you deeper into the love that makes us both whole and holy?

CHAPTER EIGHT

GET UP AND LIVE
Delighting the Lord

While he was still speaking, someone came from the leader's house to say, "Your daughter is dead; do not trouble the teacher any longer." When Jesus heard this, he replied, "Do not fear. Only believe, and she will be saved."

—LUKE 8:49–50

But he took her by the hand and called out, "Child, get up!" Her spirit returned, and she got up at once. Then he directed them to give her something to eat.

—LUKE 8:54–55

When Jesus entered Peter's house, he saw his mother-in-law lying in bed with a fever; he touched her hand, and the fever left her, and she got up and began to serve him.

—MATTHEW 8:14–15

· · · · ·

There are a few moments in my life outside the times I delivered my boys and they were baptized that I could say made me feel truly and fully alive. One occurred when I was a young girl just on the cusp of puberty. Ballet was my passion, and it was the one day every few months parents could enter and watch our class. I can't say if it was the additional eyes watching—a crowd to perform for—or if I felt extra confident that day, but there was an assuredness in the way I moved and controlled my body through that class that was ecstatically invigorating. I had never before felt, and am not sure I have ever since, so free inside my body and so able to make it do what I wanted it to do. I can still bring myself back to the memory of the sweat dripping down my back in rivulets, the feel of the snap of my head that kept my pirouettes spinning in perfect timing, the full, active extension of my arms and legs as I leapt in grand jetés across the studio. I was a girl becoming a woman, and for probably one of the last times, a girl fully alive and confident in her body.

The other moment occurred much later in our first foreign mission post on a small dot of a Caribbean island called Canouan. This particular day, I was climbing across the island over a narrow mountain path toward the village school where I would give the children catechism class for their first Communion preparation. It was hot, as Caribbean islands tend to be, and the path was rocky and treacherous, so I had to keep my eyes on the placement of my feet as I walked, turning away from my normal fixation with watching the sparkling turquoise water that surrounded the island as I walked. This day, I watched my feet intently as a layer of dust began to cover them, as I placed my leather embossed sandals, handmade by an island local, in just the right spots and traversed my way to serve the little ones to whom God had sent me as his servant, his missionary. For one single moment on that path, it was as if the veil between heaven and earth slid open, and I knew without a doubt that right then and there, I was doing exactly what God had created me to do, body and soul, in this moment of my life. It was a short-lived but profound experience that has never faded from my memory.

These moments for me are moments of wellness, of wholeness, of feeling fully alive. They are a striking contrast to the moments of hardship and suffering in my life, of the moments my body denied me healthy pregnancies or my mind denied me rational thinking, of the moments when self-loathing sent me scraping my pain out on my own skin. Yet, I am realizing I should not let the painful memories crowd these moments out, blind me to the times I felt so fully alive, or convince me that it has all been all pain, this life of mine. For God's greatest desire for our human existence is that we live it, fully alive in him. I tend to become a bit spiritually sleepy when my life is moving on at a peaceful clip and things are going fairly well. Rather than being brought to life by God's goodness that surrounds me, I can easily become complacent. Without the suffering and pain that draw me into such desperate dependence on him, my wellness can feel, well, less important.

Author Micha Boyett, in her spiritual memoir *Found*, makes a compelling point about how often God uses the word *satisfy* in Scripture to express his desire for our hearts, and we confuse it with the word *sanctify*. In seeing *sanctity* as God's desire for her, Boyett says, "I needed to 'be holy, as God is holy' and then I'd finally earn my shot at God's kindness." In contrast, discussing what it means to be satisfied in God, Boyett says, "The Spirit of God is the one who does the sanctifying. Never once...has that been my job, my job has been to seek, to look...at then say, 'Here I am. Ready to be remade.'"[12]

It is God's great delight to make us well and satisfy our hearts, and we are the best servants we can be when we have allowed him to do just that. In having our hearts made well by God, our bodily service to him is borne of a satisfied and overflowing heart that is at home with itself and the physical world it inhabits. In recognizing the many ways he satisfies us, the times that we are well become moments of feeling miraculously alive and close to him rather than a sleepy existence that fails to open its eyes and really see the great delight our Creator takes in our living.

~ CONSIDERING DELIGHT ~

What does it look like for us as women to be well—as in when we sing the refrain of the hymn "It Is Well with My Soul"? The hymn counts us well when we realize that no matter our state and no matter our sins, Jesus is there attending us, like the good physician that he is, healing us and making us well on a spiritual level. If we go back to our equation of spiritual wellness with a wellness of our bodily experience, we can also then say that being well means being fully alive to our earthly existence, awake to God's action in us and in the world around us, and elevated by it.

Often, we are not aware as adult women of the many parts of us that have become deadened to the life-giving love of Christ, of the ways we have closed our eyes and chosen slumber over really perceiving his saving action in us. We have lost touch with parts of ourselves we once delighted in, and the days in which our bodies themselves were a delight to us. We let the innocent little girl who most reflected God's image in us be deadened by our burdens, our pains, our responsibilities, or a million constricting boxes into which we have stuffed ourselves so that we could receive the affirmation and approval we desperately long for. We have, in truth, suffocated some of the truest parts of ourselves, the girls we were before we were told in one way or another that we should be something else instead. Before the message seeped deep into our souls that our sanctity lies in something more than being satisfied by God's goodness, we knew how to delight in ourselves and allow ourselves to be delighted in.

God wants to restore that delight. This is the work of the great physician on our Eden hearts, the hearts of our young, new selves, the hearts that were ours when we were most like Eve. The word *delight* appears in Scripture approximately 110 times, almost all of them in the Old Testament.[13] The God of the Old Testament is God the Father, our loving, compassionate Father, who over and over again proclaims that he delights in us (Psalms 16, 18, 22, 35).

That afternoon I spent lifting my body lithely into the air in the ballet studio, I delighted in who I was physically and also in my spirit, which had with perseverance and discipline arrived at that level of skill. And while I did not consciously think of it in that moment, I am sure now there was some awareness of the fact that I was delighted *in.* I am just beginning to learn that very attitude, that I was delighted in because of my abilities, because of my level of performance, soon became an open sore on my soul that was eventually infected with perfectionism and later festered into a soul-eating variety of obsessive compulsiveness. Not long after that day in the ballet studio, the rapid changes of puberty took over my body, and I closed my eyes to finding delight in its ability to move beautifully, eventually letting almost all delight in my physical appearance die along with it.

It is hard to define where the point is that this delightful sense of who we are begins to fade, and what aspect of ourselves it affects most. Certainly, it differs for each of us, and yet, I have heard enough stories from enough women to say I am quite sure it does happen to each of us. As we forget to take delight in ourselves, as we fall into the heavy sleep of survival, of being just enough to get by, the death of self-loathing, self-doubt, or the asphyxiation of trying to be someone we are not to gain approval, we also forget what it feels like to be delighted in. Many of us cease to believe it all together and lose the intimacy of what it means to relate to our God as a little girl to her Abba, not only in complete trust, but in wide-eyed expectation and joy. We forget what it means to be well, what it meant in Eden to be woman, innocent, free, and uncovered, taking great delight in the way the Lord made us, the way he walked beside us, and the way he provided for all our needs.

With our senses deadened to that delight, we begin to exchange his invitation to be satisfied in him for the pressure to sanctify ourselves—to perform our faith to be worthy, not of God's delight, which we have long forgotten, but of his mercy for all our imperfections. Do you see how deeply wound in lies that thought is? First, we close our eyes to the delight the Father took in creating us. Then, we refuse his invitation to know full satisfaction in him. We take in its place the burden of self-sanctification and performance to prove ourselves worthy of his love. And we replace our desire to be delighted in by the Lord with earning what we convince ourselves surely must be a begrudging mercy for all the ways we are imperfect.

It is this perversion of the intimacy we are meant to have with our Father that eats away at the vivacity of our spiritual lives and our physical experience of that life. When we die to his delight in us and to the invitation to be satisfied with the way he created us, we forget who we are. We morph into an extension of the expectations that have been heaped upon us by others and by ourselves. The shame of all the ways we fail to meet those expectations makes our eyelids heavy, makes it easier to live a sleepy half-existence rather than to pursue a life of freedom, in which we listen intently for the voice of the Father who calls to us to get up and live.

Emily Dickinson remembers her girlish joy in the poem "Delight Is as the Flight." In these four lines, she sums up what it is to be enchanted by our Father's lovely world, to be delighted by him:

> And I, for glee,
> Took Rainbows, as the common way,
> And empty Skies
> The Eccentricity—[14]

Perhaps as grown women we can no longer live in a world where we expect rainbows every day and see the plain sky as the rarity. Maybe to meet our responsibilities and live in the reality of our modern world, we need to keep our eyes open with a certain level of sensibility. On the other hand, if we consider the rainbow as the sign of God's promise of faithfulness to us, his covenant of love with humanity, why should we not wake our rainbow-loving little girls and look with expectation to the heavens for signs that our Father is dripping with delight and its sparkling dust fills the air around us?

I have a dear group of friends who have suddenly become obsessed with unicorns. These same women are also some of my favorite people to surround myself with because they are acutely aware of their Father's love for them, and it overflows in joy, in laughter, and in a sense that they know just who they are and are embracing that life with delight. There is no way for them to live that authenticity without also trusting that their Father delights in them, and that unicorns with rainbow tails and sparkly manes are a reminder of their truest hearts, the hearts they had before anything broke in them, before anything fell asleep, before anything died. They are women who have chosen to stand in bare trust before the heart of their Father and accept his invitation to get up and live, as they did in their little girl innocence, as they did when they were still Eve. We are all invited to follow their example.

~ In the Doorways of Jairus and Peter ~

I know there are many women for whom the concept of God the Father has to be extricated from wounded relationships and experiences with our own fathers. It can be hard to imagine the kind of all-encompassing, compassionate love God has for us when it doesn't match our experience of a father. Yet I am certain that since the day he blocked the gates of Eden behind Adam and Eve, God the Father has been running after his daughters, desperate for them to be well, and for them to know him as a good, good Father.

The story of Jairus's daughter from Matthew's Gospel contains my favorite words that Jesus ever spoke, life-giving words for the hearts of women. Jairus is a Jewish synagogue leader who seeks Jesus because his daughter is on the verge of death. Scripture tells us he ran to Jesus, pushing through a large crowd, and fell to his knees, begging Jesus to come lay hands on his sick daughter. Without saying a word, Jesus begins to follow him home, the crowds pushing along behind him. It is at this point that a hemorrhaging woman reaches out and touches his garment and is immediately healed (Mark 5:25–34).

Just after Jesus declares the hemorrhaging woman healed by her faith, the people who have been holding the death watch at the bedside of Jairus's little daughter arrive to announce that it is too late. She is already dead and he should not waste any more of the master's time. Jesus, though, is not deterred by their news, and instead replies to the father, "Do not fear, only believe" as he pushes on purposefully toward Jairus's house (Mark 5:36). When Jesus arrives and finds the crowd weeping and making a great commotion, he asks them why they weep when the girl is not dead but only sleeping. And they laugh at him, at Jesus— God made man, Savior of the world, maker of miracles.

Ignoring them, Jesus enters the girl's room, allowing entrance only to her father, mother, and the apostles who accompanied him. Closing out the noise of those too quick to lament this little one's death, he takes her by the hand, and calls out to her, *Talitha cum*, meaning, "Little girl, arise." She rises immediately, and he commands the family to give her something to eat (Mark 5:41).

How many of us need to know that God our Father sees the little girl inside of us who feels lifeless in so many ways, who is running out to the Son to beg that he come make us well? Imagine what it was like for Jairus, who was begging passionately for the life of his beloved daughter and instead heard what we can only presume are family members or friends arriving to announce her death and to encourage him to not waste Jesus's time on her—his child, his baby girl, whom he loves with all his heart.

Jesus is not concerned about them or the others at the house who laugh at the possibility of this little one having life left in her. He is following the heart of a father toward his little girl, and he is going to make her well again. He shuts out the noise and cynicism of the world around them and surrounds that sweet little one with only the love of her parents and the faith of his apostles, and he takes her by the hand and calls her back to life with the simplest phrase, two words, *Talitha cum*. He calls this precious daughter, so beloved by her father, he calls her to rise and to live.

We don't know what it was that made her sick or how long this little girl had been in bed suffering, but try to imagine for a moment how the scene appeared to her when she heard his voice, fluttered her eye lids open, and saw the stunned but over-joyed faces of her mother and father, and this rabbi standing there beside her bed. Had she herself known she was dead, or was she wondering about all the commotion as she awoke from what seemed a nap? Did someone have to explain it all to her later, or did she know what her father's love and faith had obtained for her from this miracle-working Jesus?

Jesus tells her to get up, and the story says she does exactly that: "immediately she got up and began to walk about" (Mark 5:42). I wonder what expression her young face wore as she looked at those who had been so quick to declare her dead. Did she flash with defiance, or was she simply too awed by being alive to worry at all what anyone else thought? Was she still a bit stunned and foggy as her spirit made its way back to her physical body and began to move about? Is that why Jesus wanted her fed, so that she could feel the sensations of her body again and know that she was fully alive? What does the first meal you eat after you die and come back to life taste like? Was it an Eden meal, like Eve's first tastes of the fruits of the garden, where her innocence allowed her to experience the delights of her senses in their perfection?

Three chapters later, in Matthew 8, there are two short verses (14–15) in which Jesus once again stands in the doorway of a home where many are begging to be healed. This time it is Peter's doorway. As he enters the house, he sees that the woman of the home, Peter's mother-in-law, is burning with fever. He reaches out and touches her hand, just like he did for that precious daughter in Jairus's home, and she is immediately healed and gets up to serve him.

This is the sequel of Jairus's daughter's story. This is the mission he has for his *Talithas*—his precious girls—who are also his Eves—his "mothers of all the living." This is his reason for desiring so intently the wellness of all the pieces of our hearts. Jesus first reaches out his hand to the little girls inside us, the core piece of our vulnerable, naked hearts, and calls them back to life so that he can then touch the adult women we are and call us into his service.

~ WAKING AND SERVING ~

Like the moment he entered the doorway of Jairus's home and set eyes on that precious one, Jesus, spurred on by the love of God our Father, looks at you with love, reaches his hand out to you, and calls you back to the full, abundant life you were meant to live. God who marked your days and laid them out like pages before him wants you to be the little girl made well, the little girl who gets up and eats, the little girl who is returned to her body healed and whole. Jesus is calling you like he called Jairus's daughter, to let your sleepy eyes flutter open, and in your womanhood, embrace and let live the little girl you were before you knew you should be anything else. Because he has a mission for you, and he needs you to be well, to be awake, to be fully alive, and to be fed so that you can do it well.

Far too often we women get this story backwards in our brains and hearts. We convince ourselves that the more we lay down our lives to serve, the more we give of ourselves and forget who we are in the name of Jesus—in the name of holiness—the healthier we will become spiritually. Or maybe we aren't even conscious of the mindset from which we are pursuing Jesus's approval. Perhaps our young hearts' wounds were inflicted so early and so often that we do not even know that we are burning up with fever. But so many of us know that we are very, very tired. Heart tired. Bone tired. Soul tired. And we are not sure why.

Just before Christmas, my missionary heart reached this level of tiredness. I knew I was unwell, that something inside me I could not identify was exhausting me, like the ache of a fever from an infection no one can find. I was a servant. I gave of myself to everyone I could. I was sure I was doing what God called me to do. And I loved the people I served and the life I lived doing it. And yet, depression and anxiety had taken such a deep hold on me that waking up in the morning to face another day made my heart beat too hard in my chest, my hands sweat, and my stomach lurch with nausea. I began, for moments at a time, to literally forget who I was. Eventually, I found myself lying in a hospital bed days before Christmas with a psychiatrist looking at me through large, empathetic eyes and explaining that I had a lot of work to do to get well. And that it would require that I stop serving others while I let myself be fed and nourished back to physical and psychological health.

I later underwent a therapeutic intensive to help me understand the root of that fever-causing infection and then a twelve-week long relapse prevention therapy plan to learn to put the tools that will bring me health into use in my life. I have not yet returned to my missionary service in our main outreach, a pregnancy hostel for indigenous women. My heart and mind are still too fragile to endure more than the average daily stresses, and sometimes even those are too much to face without help.

Much like Jairus's daughter, I am a little, vulnerable girl who has just opened her eyes and come back to life. I am still at the table being spoon-fed the nourishment I need to live. I have realized that in getting this whole being well thing backwards, I got up to serve, like Peter's mother-in-law, carrying in my heart a little girl who was still deeply wounded. Over time, extending myself further and further to give to others and forgetting myself more and more, those wounds became infected, and the fever began to burn. I was a sick little girl and a sick servant all at once. And I desperately needed Jesus to touch my hand and bring me back to life.

The Father's desire is for the heart of the little girl who lives inside every woman. He is running after her, wanting to give her life in Christ, life in abundance (John 10:10). So many of us are so busy trying so hard to be grown women well, to serve well, that we don't recognize that the fever that is making us heavy with pain has its roots in our little girl wounds that we need to heal before we can rise to serve in a truly life-giving fashion.

Before we were Peter's mother-in-law, we were Jairus's daughter, and before we were Jairus's daughter, we were Eve. Our fallen natures and the fallen world we live in steal away the perfect beauty our Father saw in us when he knitted us together body and soul. And many of us grow into womanhood either unaware of or unwilling to recognize that the heart of who we are, the deep image-bearing parts of our natures, have gone to sleep inside us. Before he ever sends Jesus to call us into his service, our Father runs to Jesus to beg him to bring his precious daughters' hearts back to life. It is from the well of that healing, which pours over into our womanly hearts and lifts the often unidentifiable burden we carry from our shoulders, that Jesus takes our hands and leads us into his service.

We are not, as we often convince ourselves, called to serve until we have given everything we have away. We are daughters called first to a life of abundant wellness, daughters who are raised from our unconsciousness by the hand of our Savior and commanded to rise and to be fed. Then we will be women who serve him from strength and health, not from a feverish pursuit of his approval.

So many of us believe we have to earn that approval with what we can give or do for God. I now know how much of my self-worth was based in what I could do in a day, how competently I could do it, and how much of it was for others and not myself. Having to embrace this period of rest and recovery has been more difficult than I ever could have imagined, even though rest is exactly what my heart was begging for. Every week I return to therapy with the same claim, "I can't do it. I can't just take care of myself and let everything else go. There is too much to be done." And yet, I know I am still fragile. Every time I get up too soon to return to serving others, I find myself woozy with the realization that I am not ready yet. I still need to sit and be nourished back to health.

In accepting that, I am beginning to see all the places my little girl heart absorbed the idea that my worth was performance-based and to see that I allowed my life to become a frenzied pursuit of competence and people-pleasing affirmation that I mistook as signs of God's love. The truth is, it is God's love that laid me down in a bed like a vulnerable little girl, took me by the hand, and called me back to life. It is God's love that is still holding me by the shoulder as, spoonful by spoonful, I consume the warmth of his mercy into my physical and spiritual being. And when I am fully restored and well, it will be with love and great delight that he touches my hand and calls me to serve again.

We women are not called to live a life of servitude to a demanding Father. We are his daughters whom he wants to heal and feed, then lift into service as evidence of his great love and delight in us. Let us not confuse the two any longer but open our sleeping eyes and be fed so that we might serve him from the fullness of our hearts and our confidence in his love.

~ MARGARET'S STORY ~

I am very proud to be a young woman growing up in our society. Countless advancements have been made to increase and encourage equality between men and women. Slowly but surely, we are closing the wage gap, and there are more and more women entering the professional world. There are female doctors, lawyers, politicians, actresses, and even women running for president. A whole movement is dedicated to equality between the sexes. Women are encouraged to be strong, independent, self-sufficient, and educated.

The paradox, as I have learned, is that our society doesn't really want women to authentically possess all those qualities. Society wants women—especially young women like me—to fit into its idea of strength and independence. If a woman is genuinely strong and intelligent, she is seen as arrogant and outspoken. We are encouraged to make our own decisions about our education, career, and sexuality but are pressured to dress, act, and talk a certain way. Women complain about disrespect from men, but our culture tells us to expose our bodies through provocative clothing and behavior. Modesty, chastity, confidence, and true intelligence are foreign ideas to our culture's idea of a modern woman. Our society is obsessed with the idea of a strong woman—as long as she remains only an idea.

I feel like it's a pretty bitter irony that I already know the hardships of being a strong woman at just seventeen. My teen years are filled with instances of me showing real strength and then being judged for it. I really struggled with this until last summer when I went on a weeklong LifeTeen retreat in the mountains of Dahlonega, Georgia.

This was undoubtedly one of the greatest weeks of my life. One of the best parts was the women's talk. Normally, I really dislike women's talks on retreats. I'm not particularly girly, and they always seem to be about how we're God's little princesses. Eww. But this talk was different. The speaker told us that as young women of God, we have inviolable and inherent dignity.

Though this emphasis on our inherent worth is something I had been taught, I never before realized the impact it makes on other people to truly believe this. The speaker's words called to mind my mom, teachers, friends, and other women who strive for and model feminine strength because they know they have inherent dignity in God.

When we live out what it really means to be strong women, we teach our daughters, sisters, and friends that their worth comes from God, and genuine confidence follows. We give them the tools they need to always be brave, wise, and articulate so that they won't just agree with the culture when their conscience tells them something is wrong. Be a strong woman yourself, and your strength will point others to God.

~ Further Up and Further In ~

Spend some time with the stories of Jairus's daughter, the hemorrhaging woman, and Peter's mother-in-law in the Gospel of Mark, chapter 5, and the Gospel of Matthew, chapter 8. How do these stories reveal a continuum of healing Jesus desires for women's hearts?

Do you have a particularly joyful memory of yourself as a young girl? What brought you such joy? Do you think you still experience joy in yourself like you did as a girl? Why or why not?

Where does your sense of self-worth come from? Do you see yourself as a delight to your heavenly Father in your very existence? Are there ways you base your worth on what you can do for God?

What aspects of your heart might Jesus want to heal and bring back to life? How might he desire for you to sit and allow yourself to be fed rather than jumping up to serve?

CHAPTER NINE

CONSUMMATE LOVE

Espoused for Eternity

Draw me after you, let us make haste.
  The king has brought me into his chambers.
We will exult and rejoice in you;
  we will extol your love more than wine;
  rightly do they love you.
—SONG OF SOLOMON 1:4

My beloved speaks and says to me:
"Arise, my love, my dove, my fair one,
  and come away;
for behold the winter is past,
  the rain is over and gone.
The flowers appear on the earth,
  the time of pruning has come,
and the voice of the turtledove
  is heard in our land."
—SONG OF SOLOMON 2:10–12

Who is that coming up from the wilderness,
leaning upon her beloved?
Under the apple tree I awakened you.
There your mother was in labor with you;
there she who bore you was in labor.

Set me as a seal upon your heart,
as a seal upon your arm,
for love is strong as death,
jealousy is cruel as the grave.
Its flashes are flashes of fire,
a most vehement flame.

—SONG OF SOLOMON 8:5–6

· · · · ·

I know many people who find funerals, even for people who are only acquaintances, difficult and anxiety provoking. I know others who find even talking about death unsettling. For me, I have found funerals some of the most comforting, consoling moments of my life, even the most difficult of them. At my son Bryce's funeral, I remember reaching out to touch his tiny casket with one hand as I received the Eucharist. In that particular circumstance, when the death of my son could not be changed, I could not imagine any other thing on earth more intimately and profoundly consoling than to hand him over to God as the ancient words and wisdom of the Church were spoken over us both in the funeral rite, and then to receive communion while I shared one last earthly embrace, in the form of that outstretched hand on his coffin, with my son.

I don't know if it is because I experienced deaths of loved ones, grandparents and other family members, early on and with odd frequency in my life, or because I am just wired a little differently than many people—I mean I do take mood stabilizers to try to keep my obsessive dark thoughts away—but pondering death and our mortality has never felt strange or scary to me—grief, yes. but death itself, not so much. And pondering heaven and eternity has been a source of imaginative delight and curious wonder for me for most of my life.

Over the years, the form heaven takes in my mind has changed. When I was a little girl, I imagined myself twirling in the twirliest, whitest dress ever in a lush green field full of wildflowers and flitting yellow butterflies. In my adolescence, it was the thought of no more crying and no more pain that drew me to heaven, imagining myself at total peace beside a river, sitting in the shade of a tree with Jesus by my side, tenderly embracing me.

As I grew to adulthood, I tried to embrace the theological truth that heaven is not a place, but the state in which my soul would be at union with God after death if I had merited salvation by faith and grace. And yet, I still thought about being reunited with my own father, about seeing the streets of gold, and about sitting beside some of my favorite saints to thank them for their friendship and intercession.

When I buried my baby son and then lost four more children to miscarriage, my view of heaven became deeply influenced by the longing to hold my babies in my arms once again. I still have so much hope in heaven as the place where I will feel the weight of my little saints against my chest.

No matter how much I try to contemplate the concept of heaven without a physical reality, it seems I can't *not* see it as a place, with the souls that inhabit it as people, and the God with whom I will experience full communion as the incarnated Jesus. I can't extract my longing for eternity from my experiences in the physical world inside a human body.

I am not trying to talk myself out of it anymore, because that vision and longing for heaven as a physical paradise and a bodily reality, is, in fact, the final state the universe will reach when God comes again and reunites the world fully to himself, restoring it to its original goodness and glory. In that moment, each of the souls in heaven will also be restored to a physical body in its perfect state.

It is wonderful to think that the end of all our Eden longings, the end of all our desires to return to that perfect harmony we knew with God, his creation, ourselves, and others, will come to fruition at the end of time. First, we have the hope that salvation in Christ and the life of grace in the Church will lead us to a spiritual consummation of our love of God in heaven. From that perfect spiritual state, we will await with joy the moment when all the physical world, including our human bodies, are brought into their full glory too.

St. Teresa Benedicta of the Cross wrote to women, "We cannot evade the question of who we are and what we should be." If we are believers in the goodness of a God who created us to belong to him and live in perfect love with him, then we know that the full truth of who we are and what we should be as women can only be the final spiritual union with him we hope to enjoy in heaven, and then the final glory of the whole universe being elevated to its original state, where our souls and bodies will once again live in the fullness of their Eden perfection. All of life between today and that point must be informed by that hope, so who we are as women is defined by our eternal perspective. How we love God, this world, ourselves, and others must reflect clearly that we believe there is a bit of the divine image imprinted on every human soul and every aspect of creation and that one day we will see that image in its full glory.

If this is who we are, then who we should be is easily defined. We are women who reach for that harmony in every way possible while we inhabit this earth in physical bodies, who live to develop deeper intimacy with God and in learning to love him more deeply, learn also to love ourselves and others more deeply. We are women who long to embrace our creational, incarnational, and relational capacities, choosing vulnerability and intimacy over hiddenness and shame as we await the day we can walk freely again inside our bodies in consummate love with our Creator, the second coming of our Eden paradise.

~ Considering Consummation ~

For a long time, it was difficult for me to read the scriptural images of God calling humanity—his people and our individual souls—beloved or espoused in a clearly marital sense. The idea of such intimate spiritual communion with God triggered in me an impulse to draw back, mainly because it made me feel desired in a way that demanded my nakedness, my vulnerability, and my acceptance of his consummate love. And that felt off-putting to me, like a little *too much* love.

Yet any of us desiring a relationship with God are also undoubtedly desiring to spend eternity with him in heaven; that hope draws us to his love and mercy. And the state we aim for in heaven is that deep, intimate communion I shy away from when I hear about it through earthly ears. Our ultimate goal is to fully consummate our love with our beloved and be espoused by him, for our souls to be joined to God in a perfect union for eternity.

Looking more closely at the meaning of the word *consummate*, it becomes less off-putting. *Con* is a familiar prefix meaning "with," but that could also be interpreted to mean "the joining of two things." *Summa*, the root of the word, means "the highest form of something," and *ate* or *ation* are both suffixes indicating action.[15] So consummate love, then, is the act of loving that joins things together into their highest form. God, of course, is unchanging, so he exists eternally in his highest form. It is we who are elevated by receiving and returning this consummate love of God.

When our souls are joined to him in the final, eternal communion of heaven, we will reach the highest form of ourselves in the height of love with God. This spiritual union with our Creator will return us to the perfect state of connection and harmony we were made to enjoy with him when he created us and imagined us into being. All stain of our concupiscence purged, we will be able to bare our souls before him in that perfect vulnerability that was our Eden nakedness and be espoused by him, joined to him in an eternal, intimate embrace of complete communion that the love of spouses is meant to imitate in its earthly form.

The *Catechism of the Catholic Church* speaks of this heavenly consummation in this way:

> *For man,* this consummation will be the final realization of the unity of the human race, which God willed from creation and of which the pilgrim Church has been "in the nature of sacrament." Those who are united with Christ will form the community of the redeemed, "the holy city" of God, "the Bride, the wife of the Lamb." She will not be wounded any longer by sin, stains, self-love, that destroy or wound the earthly community. The beatific vision, in which God opens himself in an inexhaustible way to the elect, will be the ever-flowing well-spring of happiness, peace, and mutual communion. (CCC, 1045)

We spend our earthly lives trying to return to God the perfect love he offers us through the fog of our souls' imperfections. We get glimpses of the beauty of his mercy, his compassion, and his love for us that spur us on in running the race toward our ultimate union with him. Our hearts are compelled to long for that union, even in the times it seems we are rejecting his love and turning away from him. Because we were made by God and for God, we can never fully impede our heart's longing to accept and return his love for us, no matter how much our own wounds cause us to turn our backs from that love or keep an unhealthy wall of indifference around our hearts.

Those states of distance and separation most likely indicate an acute, if subconscious, awareness of that longing, which our sense of shame and unworthiness causes us to hide from, just as Eve reacted to her own sin in Eden. But long for his consummate love we do, for we are exactly designed to do so. Our life on earth, if we are earnestly pursuing the Trinitarian life of faith, is an ever-further reaching for intimacy with our God that creates a deeper craving to live in the eternal perfection of love with him. To achieve the pinnacle of love with our beloved, akin to spousal intimacy in the depths of its joining of our souls to his, God will pour out his perfect love to us inexhaustibly, and we will be eternally satisfied by returning that love.

Considering this truth, my initial reaction to shy away from such a notion of union with God fades, and like a young woman excited by the first notions of love, I blush with emotion and longing rather than a sense of unworthiness and shame. God comes to pursue and woo me into love with him during my earthly days so he may one day claim me fully as his own, embracing me in the Eden embrace my heart was created to know.

A picture from my wedding nearly twenty years ago will always be a favorite for the memory it evokes. My husband and I stand in the embrace of our first dance as a married couple. He smiles mischievously, as I lean my head into his chest with a rose blush creeping up my neck into my cheeks and a shyness in my smile. He had alluded to what would come when we could retire from the crowd at that party and finally be alone together, and I had vulnerably shown him my combined joy and slight trepidation at the thought of his desire for me.

Our relationship with God during our earthly lives is much like that first dance. We fall ever deeper in love with him as we accept his love for us, until finally, we are hand in hand, heart to heart, drawn in to him, and moving in unison with his will, returning the love he has offered us. At the end of our lives, if we have fully accepted that love, we leave the dance floor and the crowded party to be swept away into the intimate embrace of consummate love, espoused forever to our God, truly naked before him in spirit, and rejoicing in the eternal ecstasy of that union.

Yes, God desires us as a bridegroom longs for his young bride. And we need not be shy to know his longing or feel ashamed to be so deeply desired. We need simply to let ourselves be wooed by him as we bask in his love, knowing that it is in that reception that we will be led by his hand into an eternity of inexhaustible union with our Creator. The Eden instinct that has drawn us to the notion of perfect harmony with him during our earthly lives will become a reality.

~ BACK TO THE GARDEN WITH THE BELOVED ~

The United States Conference of Catholic Bishops, in its introduction text on the Song of Solomon says:

> The Song of [Solomon] (or Canticle of Canticles) is
> an exquisite collection of love lyrics, arranged to tell a
> dramatic tale of mutual desire and courtship...the Song
> has been read as a sublime portrayal and praise of this
> mutual love of the Lord and his people. Christian writers
> have interpreted the Song in terms of the union between
> Christ and the Church and of the union between Christ
> and the individual soul.[16]

This epic love song of the soul on the lookout for the coming of
her beloved is a song of desire, of courtship—the Lord wooing
us up into eternity with him as we call unto him to come and
retrieve us and claim us as his own. We sing out to him as part
of his whole Church body and we sing out to him individually,
our own souls personally longing for our beloved.

A constant exchange between the two lovers, we women sing
out to our God, and he in turn responds to us. We cry out to
him as we await his coming and sing back his love for us. There
is no less longing in his song to us than there is in ours to him.
We initiate the song, begging him to "draw me after you, let
us make haste" so we may "exult and rejoice in you." We sing
with the host of souls who also extol him, acknowledging that
"rightly do they love [him]" (Song of Solomon 1:4). How often
have I found myself in prayer, begging the Lord to come, to just
hurry up and come, not even sure what was I really praying for,
whether it was a longing to feel his nearness now, or a literal
longing for him to come and redeem this wounded world we

live in. Regardless, long for him I do, and I often cry out to him with the same urgency of this love song, my soul urging his closeness, longing to touch him, so that I will be released from the painful longing and into the song of praise sung by the choir of the redeemed.

And the Lord, hearing our song of love and longing responds, telling us where to find him: "Follow in the tracks of the flock" to him, "beside the shepherds' tents" (Song of Solomon 1:8) The Good Shepherd, the one who tends our hearts, calls us to him in the pasture of his flock, offering us the tracks laid by those who have gone before us as a path to follow to him. We are called not as sheep of the flock, as we are here on earth, but elevated to his betrothed, his beloved bride he longs to consummate himself to. He looks at us and sings out his own desire, his longing for our souls: "Ah, you are beautiful, my love, ah, you are beautiful." (Song of Solomon 1:15)

It is not often that I go to prayer, close my eyes, and just let the love of the Lord wash over me, hear him sing his longing for my heart, and accept his declaration of my beauty. Yet this is the song of one returning to the garden of Paradise, one who remembers who she was in Eden, the song of those who trust we were made in love and for love. Even though our fallen bodies have turned away from that love many times, if we cleanse our souls with the fragrance of his mercy, he looks at us and sees the beauty he did in Eden. He longs to embrace us and sing intimately into our ears how beautiful he thinks we really are, how much he desires to unite with us in an eternal communion.

We return again to our singing, to our calling out, a call of the waiting hearts, who sit outside in the garden in the shade of his lovely creation, recognizing that his intent for us is love, and that he will feed us at his banqueting table until we are full, satiated, satisfied in him. We wait on earth with this longing. Sometimes we forget what we long for, we forget that what we await is love and full satisfaction in our God. Sometimes we convince ourselves that we sit waiting for him to chastise, or waiting for him to weep with us over the state of our souls, but our earthly work, the work that makes our waiting souls ready and beautiful for him, is our expectation of his love, our hunger to be satisfied in him, our own desire to consummate ourselves in love. It is this expectation that calls us to obey him, to wait with patience for him until we see him coming for us—surrendered in faith to the reality that he will indeed come in his time and that he will come only with the intent to love us. We begin to undress our souls before him, waiting bared and surrendered to full trust in his intention to love us.

Finally, the Bridegroom will call to us to arise and come, just as he did so many times in the person of Jesus when he called a sick or suffering soul to arise and come to him. Just as he does for us when he offers himself as sacrifice on the altar and then calls for us to literally rise and come to receive him, to commune with him, to consume him. He will call from behind the veil for us to arise and come for the final time. Having allowed him to heal our broken hearts with the grace of his touch and the sacraments that unite us to his beloved bride, the Church, we will be ready to heed the call and run to him, over the mountains, our souls knowing that our "beloved is ours and [we are] his," confident that as we live "until the day breaks and the shadows flee," we can express our deepest longings for love to him, and he will come running to meet them, "like a gazelle" leaping over the mountains (Song of Solomon 2:16–17).

And so the exchange goes, the longing heart of our God for us and ours for him, until the moment he finally arrives and declares his unrelenting love: "You have ravished my heart, my sister, my bride, you have ravished my heart with a glance of your eyes.... How sweet is your love, my sister, my bride!" (Song of Solomon 4:9–10). Our God reminds us that he has been ravished with love for us since the day the garden gates closed and our intimate union was broken. He has looked upon us with a deep desire to return to that union, and each time we have returned the look of love, his heart has flooded with even more love for us.

So we sing our canticle of love to our God with our lives, and he to us with his saving love until, at last, we are brought into the full consummation of that love for eternity. We will approach Paradise "leaning upon our beloved," redeemed by a love "strong as death, a passion fierce as the grave" (Song of Solomon 8:5–6), until we return to the garden, and walk once again naked and unashamed with our God, all our longings now fulfilled, singing the ecstatic song of "Hosanna, Hosanna, Hosanna in the highest."

~ Bringing Our Bodies Back to Us ~

The *Catechism of the Catholic Church*, speaking of the final triumph of Christ, when he comes to redeem the earth and all that is in it, reminds us that "At the end of time, the Kingdom of God will come in its fullness. After the universal judgment, the righteous will reign forever with Christ, glorified in body and soul. The universe itself will be renewed" (CCC, 1042).

It is hard to believe that even after we experience the consummate love of our God on a spiritual level and are assured that we will enjoy the ecstasy of that love for eternity, there is still more glory to come. But, oh there is! Because on the day the Lord's reign comes to fulfillment and the whole universe is renewed, restored again to its original, untainted glory, our earthly bodies will experience the same renewal and be restored to us, reuniting the two aspects of our selves, body and soul, in the perfection of the Kingdom fully come.

Some of the most gorgeous hope I have ever witnessed was at the funerals of children who had lived in bodies that suffered through physical and mental disability. Always their parents and families, even as they grieve, relish the thought of them free from the limitations of those bodies and able to be fully alive before God. Usually that joy is translated into a bodily experience, a vision of their child, who lived untainted by sin because their limited abilities kept them unable to choose anything but love, running freely through lush green fields into the arms of God, dancing, throwing a head back in wild laughter, seeing colors for the first time, or singing in perfect harmony the song of the saints.

They are so right to embrace and imagine this hope. We can all share the belief that one day our bodies will be ours again, and we will know what it was like to be woman in the Garden of Paradise because we will live that life forever under the triumphant reign of God. This is why we are free from all obligation to feel shame for our bodies while we inhabit them on earth, to take in the world's message that in our physical forms we are never enough and also too much, that the care of them is selfish, while the sacrifice of their well-being is holy.

God not only does not hate our bodies, but awaits the moment when the heavens and the earth will be glorified in him and our bodies will be returned to us—the ultimate act of his great love for his creation.

The Church tell us that "far from diminishing our concern to develop this earth, the expectancy of a new earth should spur us on, for it is here that the body of a new human family grows, foreshadowing in some way the age which is to come" (CCC, 642). We can extend that same belief to developing our relationship to our human bodies, knowing that in our "concern to develop" a healthy relationship with them, we are expressing "our expectancy of a new earth" that "spurs us on" to love God's creation, including ourselves, our ever-real, incarnate, bodily selves, which are part of that creation.

Our earthly work of caring for creation as the home he granted us, ourselves as his image bearers, and our neighbors as our family in him, is a harbinger of the eternal reality to come— the reality that will be realized first as spiritual triumph and, one day, as physical triumph as well. What more permission do we need to see our bodies as a vital and integral part of our lives in Christ, of our salvation, than the knowledge that in the ultimate reign of God, he will hand them back to us in their glorified state and exult in us as we rejoice at their return!

The Catechism goes on to say, "When we have spread on earth the fruits of our nature and our enterprise...according to the command of the Lord and in his Spirit, we will find them once again, cleansed this time from the stain of sin, illuminated and transfigured, when Christ presents to his Father an eternal and universal kingdom" (CCC, 1050). Imagine the moment when the Holy Spirit moves across the world we have created with our incarnational bodies, creational intellects, and relational love and points out the fruits of those efforts to Jesus, who then gathers them along with the bodies that created them, and presents it all to his Father to become part of the eternal kingdom, the kingdom that encompasses all things.

We can have no greater hope than this. It is a tangible, physical hope, the end of the story that began in Eden, when we were all Eve, and ends—we believe in faith—with a new paradise filled with glorified female bodies released from every sin and stain and fully free in their nakedness to adore their God, his creation, themselves, and one another in the triumphant victory. Every peeling away of the falseness of shame we accomplish here on earth, every vulnerable peeking out of our spiritual nakedness, is a hint of that life to come, and it is the spark that ignites our passion to return to Eden and live the consummate love of our Creator. Growing trust in our Eden instinct is a sign of our growing belief that God's desire for us and our desire to present ourselves "holy and blameless in love before him," knowing that the union of those desires will one day bring us fully back to ourselves in eternal ecstasy.

~ MARY'S STORY ~

The moment my daughter Courtney bore down like a locomotive at full speed during my labor, and the OB nurses screamed at me as my body collapsed under the assault, I felt like a failure. Childbirth was supposed to be less complicated than this. Even today, twenty-five years later, I remember trying to control my unwieldy body, concentrating on breathing in and out to relieve the pain, as my daughter struggled to enter the world, being reminded constantly of the war I had always fought with my body.

Moments after her birth, Courtney's fuzzy head nestled over my racing heart, her legs tucked up, she breathed gently and was content while my arms protected her from harm. I figured that while I'd had a difficult delivery, I would have the physical strength to take care of this tiny girl and her toddler brother. I was at peace with myself.

Little did I know that peace wouldn't last. A few weeks later, the seizures started. Courtney's body collapsed in on itself, writhing in pain and confusion. When the shaking stopped and her breathing settled, I scooped her up, her head on my chest, and wrapped her in my arms. Despite the truth of the seizures, I felt like harm couldn't come to her there. I felt like my body could protect her. We would live this rhythm of her body collapsing and mine comforting her for twenty-two more years.

As Courtney grew, I entered a new kind of body war. While I would never shame another woman about her weight, somehow, I believed it was okay to feel shame about mine. Because the truth is that my weight gain and loss of muscle strength directly impacted how I could care for both my children. There were days when I couldn't get out of the chair with Courtney in my arms or lift her into her bed, days when I couldn't get onto the floor to play Legos with my son.

I was caught in a vicious cycle of self-hatred and guilt. Since the medications for the seizures took away Courtney's sight and balance, and the brain damage from them destroyed her muscles, I became her hands and feet. Unfortunately, that meant that my arms were always burning and that my back screamed in pain. I pushed through in loving service for her, but had to face a terrible truth. All of my own physical and emotional pain was self-inflicted. While I had the power to change my physical situation, I was mentally and emotionally incapable of doing so.

As time wore both of our bodies down, and I realized Courtney's days here were short, I discovered that despite my physical limitations, I'd always been Courtney's safe harbor. For years, I'd carried and held and protected her. Regardless of my weight, I'd done the best I could do for her. And it was time to lay away the guilt and the shame.

After Courtney's death, a gentle change came over me. Guilt was replaced by gratitude and shame overshadowed by grace. The drums of war quieted, and despite my grief, my heart was at peace. I'd accepted my body for what it was and am proud of what it accomplished. With my body and all its imperfections, I had loved and loved well. And that is enough.

~ FURTHER UP AND FURTHER IN ~

What is your relationship with the idea of death and mortality? How does your relationship with God affect your views? How do your views affect your relationship with God?

How do you respond to the idea of God relating to us as a lover? What does his consummate love mean to you?

Have you ever thought about what it will be like to be reunited to your physical body at the end of time? What is triumphant about this idea?

Imagine your glorified body in a glorified earth. Pray or write a prayer of thanksgiving to God for the spiritual hope of heaven and the hope of final glorification of the physical world.

CHAPTER TEN

∘∘∘

SACRISTANS OF OUR OWN TEMPLES

Blessings and Benedictions for Your Body

God the Father of our Lord Jesus Christ has freed you from sin, given you a new birth by water and the Holy Spirit, and welcomed you into his holy people. He now anoints you with the chrism of salvation. As Christ was anointed Priest, Prophet, and King, so may you live always as a member of his body, sharing everlasting life.

—FROM THE RITE OF BAPTISM

Lord Jesus Christ, our Redeemer, by the grace of your Holy Spirit cure the weakness of your servant. Heal his/her sickness and forgive his/her sins; expel all afflictions of mind and body; mercifully restore him/her to full health, and enable him/her to resume his/her former duties, for you are Lord for ever and ever.

—FROM THE RITE OF ANOINTING

This is the will of the one who sent me, says the Lord that I should not lose anything of what he gave me, but that I should raise it on the last day.

—JOHN 6:39, cited in the *Catholic Rite of Committal*

· · · · ·

I sat tucked into the corner of the couch in the soft white living room looking across at the face of a new friend as we shared the stories of our body battles. I told her of my burnout, my habit of internalizing the stress of everyone around me and engaging in self-harming behaviors, how my struggle with weight has made me feel unacceptable since my teen years. She touched the healing cuts that ran across my shoulders in a sudden awareness as she passed by me on her way back from the bathroom. She told me how she too had battled body image problems because of her weight and size since she was very young, how her dad had taken her to her first weight-loss program before she was out of elementary school, how over the past few years she had punished herself relentlessly with expensive boot camp exercise programs, feeling the relief of losing weight and then the shame of regaining it.

We both shared our stories of how the year of mercy declared by Pope Francis had brought us the unexpected lesson of hearing God speak clearly that he wanted us to have mercy on our bodies. She told me how she suddenly felt called to stop pushing the boulder of her weight uphill and to let it slide back down over her, like the mythological Sisyphus. She said she brought her pain and frustration to God and he offered her freedom in his merciful love, and simply asked, "Will you be fat for me?"—the meaning indicating, "Will you simply be who I made you to be for me?" She told me how one night, she finally surrendered her battle and let God have her, just as she was. She stood in the shower and prayed a blessing over every part of her body as she washed it: "Thank you, God, for these arms that serve you and my family daily. Thank you, God, for this voice that sings your praise. Thank you, God, for these eyes that reflect your love..."

A couple of days later, I watched that friend stand on a stage and tell this same story to an auditorium full of women—vulnerable, stripping away her veneer of perfection and baring herself to them—and I felt the room fill with a silent but palpable sigh of relief, of women's hearts letting out a nearly audible, "You too?"

My great hope is that every one of those women, in that sigh of relief, also remembered the permission to bless their bodies in love and mercy as this friend had done. I hope all of you, as readers of this book, arrive at its end with the same permission.

St. Paul calls our bodies "temples of the Holy Spirit," and as baptized members of the church, we are all incorporated into Christ's priestly calling (1 Corinthians 6:19). What if we took that figurative calling as women and gave ourselves permission to be the caretakers of our bodily temples, the sacristans of the sacred space in which we live our spiritual lives? What if we stopped thinking of the call "to present your bodies as living sacrifice, holy and acceptable to God" as a call to give ourselves away to the point of our own detriment, and remembered that this call begins with the phrase "by the mercies of God" (Romans 12:1)? His mercy makes our bodies holy and acceptable, and perhaps the sacrifice required is in caring for these bodies so that they can be made an offering to him as honored creations.

I have cited at the beginning of this chapter phrases from various sacramental rites of the Church that affirm that permission with words that our mother the Church, Christ's beloved bride, the body of which we are members, proclaims over us in her wisdom, declaring the goodness of our bodies and offering them blessing and benediction.

What follows in this chapter are blessings, benedictions, meditations, and prayers that can serve as inspiration and examples for you as you rise to the role of priest and keeper of your holy, bodily temple. My hope is that you will let them waft up like the incense that purifies the altar of offering as you surrender yourself, body and soul, to the consummate love of our God. My hope is that, as you assimilate the ideas in this book, you will begin to see your body as a blessing, as the answer to what it means to be woman, and strip away whatever has served as your fig leaf of shame, returning to a willing dependence on God and his mercy. Your nakedness reminds you of who you were when you were Eve, and who you will be when the Kingdom of God reigns for eternity—united forever in your body and soul to the perfect love of the Father in the glorious wonder of a universe fully redeemed and restored.

~ Blessings and Benedictions ~
A Litany of Thanksgiving for Your Body

I encourage you to pray this prayer at a time when you can go slowly, in quiet and full privacy, offering a loving touch to each part of your body as you move through the prayer.

Lord have mercy on my body.
Christ have mercy on my soul.
Lord have mercy on my mind and emotions.
Christ hear me.
Christ graciously hear me.
God the Father, Creator of my body, have mercy on me.
Jesus Christ, Incarnate Lord, have mercy on me.
Holy Spirit, who overshadows me in love, have mercy on me.

For these hairs of my head which you have counted strand by strand, I thank you, O Lord.

For these eyes that take in the beauty of your presence around me, I thank you, O Lord.

For these lips that speak your praise and lift my heart to you, I thank you, O Lord.

For this mouth that tastes your goodness and is satisfied by your hand, I thank you, O Lord.

For this chest that safely houses the heart that pumps life through this body, I thank you, O Lord.

For these shoulders that bear a burden that is easy and a yoke that is light because of your mercy, I thank you, O Lord.

For these arms that embrace life and express love in so many ways, I thank you, O Lord.

For these hands that create and beautify, love and serve, I thank you, O Lord.

For these breasts that remind me I am made to be a nourisher and nurturer of life, I thank you, O Lord.

For this abdomen that has been both blessing and battle-ground, and the scars it bears, I thank you, O Lord.

For the parts of me that mark me as woman and connect my body to the cycles of life, I thank you, O Lord.

For these strong legs that let me stand before all that life brings with confident hope, I thank you, O Lord.

For these feet that take me where you lead, I thank you, O Lord.

Lamb of God, who takes away the sins of my disordered passions, spare me, O Lord.

Lamb of God, who takes away the sins of my self-hatred and dissatisfaction, spare me, O Lord.

Lamb of God, who takes away the sins of my self-neglect and misperceptions, spare me, O Lord.

Almighty and eternal God, maker and lover of my soul, look upon these praises and give me new love for this body you have given me, animated by the movement of your Spirit to live in your grace and compassion, and grant that one day this body shall know the glory of your eternal triumph as it meets my soul in heaven, where you reign forever and ever. Amen.

A Psalm of Praise for How You Are Made

This prayer is a recitation of and response to Psalm 139:13–18 from The Message *(Catholic Edition) translation of the Bible. It is good to pray when you need to remember your own goodness, and that you are loved and wanted by God.*

Read: "Oh yes, you shaped me first inside, then out."

Respond: Cell by cell, you shaped me, O God. There is nothing I need to hide from you because you know every part of me. You shaped my body over my inmost parts in a unique reflection of you.

Read: "You formed me in my mother's womb."

Respond: I was wanted by you from the beginning. No one else's approval or disapproval of who I am matters because it is your eternal wisdom and perfect love that has formed me.

Read: "I thank you, High God—you're breathtaking!"

Respond: Breathtaking not only for being the good God you are, but for the way you made me. How hard it is for me to say. But, yes, I thank you, high God, for me, for every stitch and cell you took such care in creating to make me who I am. You are breathtaking, God, in your creative love and your goodness to me.

Read: "Body and soul, I am marvelously made! I worship in adoration—what a creation!"

Respond: I will say it, Lord, and I pray for the faith to believe it more each day: I am a marvel of your creation, made body and soul in your image, and I bear the fingerprints of your love over every part of me. I will adore you, God, for the marvel you have made of me. What a creation I am, indeed.

Read: "You know me inside and out,

you know every bone in my body;

You know exactly how I was made, bit by bit,

how I was sculpted from nothing into something."

Respond: No thought of mine, no imperfection, no fault, no doubt, no uncertainty has to be hidden from you, O Lord, because you know every bit of me, every synapse and connection, every thought process and flow of my emotions, how I move and what moves me. You know all of me, because it was you who took the blankness of nothing and turned it into me!

Read: "Like an open book, you watched me grow from conception to birth;

all the stages of my life were spread out before you."

Respond: Lord, free me from the thought that I need to hide any aspect of myself or my life from you. You have already read my whole story. You are the author of my life. My imperfections are no reason to hide because rather than repel you, they draw you to me, my rescuer and Redeemer. I am an open book before you, Lord. I trust you to write a love story with my life.

Read: "The days of my life all prepared before I'd even lived one day."

Respond: The days of my life were not only counted or granted or haphazardly thrown out before me, but prepared by you, O God, each one a gift burgeoning with grace, the opportunity to see you in action in and around me, and love you in return for your great love. Thank you, Lord, for the preparation you made for the days of my life, I will use them to praise you.

Read: "Your thoughts—how rare, how beautiful! God, I'll never comprehend them!"

Respond: Yes, Lord, I will never comprehend the thoughts that went into your making of me, but I will live in the trust that they were the rare and beautiful execution of your perfect, creative will that desired my existence, and I will ponder their goodness all my days.

Amen.

An Anointing of the "Ugly" Places

Take the time pray this short prayer when you are finding yourself critical of your appearance or certain aspects of your body, or when you lack confidence. If it possible, use holy oil, some comforting essential oils or coconut oil, to bless that part of your body as you finish your prayer.

My Dearest Abba,

See this part of me, right here? I want to believe you made it and you meant it to be as it is, but I look at it, Lord, and I cannot imagine that could be true. There is nothing here that seems to reflect your beauty, or any beauty at all. Give me your eyes to see me as you see me, even this detail that it seems you may have overlooked. Erase the criticism in my mind, and let me hear you declare your delight at my being and my body, you, my Father, who rejoices over me in love. Lord, I know that your thoughts cannot even contain the word *ugly*, for you are all that is good and lovely and holy. And so, if it was those thoughts that brought every bit of me into existence, I bless this part I am tempted to see as ugly, and in its anointing, reclaim it as good, as lovely, as spotless in your sight. I surrender the thought of *ugly* to you, and declare this detail of my body as marvelously and wonderfully made by your hands. In your mercy, I will believe. Help my unbelief. Amen.

A Benediction of Your Sexuality

For married or single women, this benediction is a reminder of the goodness of your sexuality and a pledge to maintain it as God intended.

I bless you, desires of my heart, longings of my soul, that call me to communion and intimate love with others.

I name you holy and righteous, and pledge myself to offer you as such as I am called to in my state of life.

I relish the capacity for pleasure you offer me and the vulnerability you ask of me.

You are gift and treasure, and no shame shall rob me of the God-granted joy I take in expressing you.

God grants me grace to use you according to his good purposes, and I assent to his will for you.

Let us go together in peace to love and serve the Lord and others together in harmony.

Thanks be to God.

A Scriptural Offering of Self-Acceptance

For every day or any day that you need to remember how to love yourself, body and soul, praying these Scriptures rhythmically and repeatedly can help ease you away from self-hatred and toward self-acceptance.

"The Lord will guide you continually, and satisfy your needs in parched places,

and make your bones strong; and you shall be like a

watered garden, like a spring of water whose waters never fail."

—ISAIAH 58:11

"Arise, shine; for your light has come, and the glory of the Lord has risen upon you.

For darkness shall cover the earth, and thick darkness the peoples; but the Lord will arise upon

you, and his glory will appear over you."

—ISAIAH 60:1–2

"Whereas you have been forsaken and hated,

with no one passing through,

I will make you majestic forever,

a joy from age to age."

—ISAIAH 60:15

"Because their shame was double, and dishonor was proclaimed as their lot,

therefore they shall possess a double portion; everlasting joy shall be theirs."

—ISAIAH 61:7

"I will greatly rejoice in the Lord, my whole being shall exult in my God; for he has clothed me with the garments of salvation, he has covered me with the robe of righteousness."

—ISAIAH 61:10

"You shall be called by a new name that the mouth of the Lord will give. You shall be a crown of beauty in the hand of the Lord, and a royal diadem in the hand of your God. You shall no more be termed Forsaken, and your land shall no more be termed Desolate; but you shall be called My Delight Is in Her, and your land Married; for the Lord delights in you."

—ISAIAH 62:2–4

"It was no messenger or angel but his presence that saved them; in his love and in his pity he redeemed them; he lifted them up and carried them."

—ISAIAH 63:9

"O Lord, you are our Father;
  we are the clay, and you are our potter;
  we are all the work of your hand."

—ISAIAH 64:8

"As a mother comforts her child, so I will comfort you; you shall be comforted."

—ISAIAH 66:13

"You shall see, and your heart shall rejoice; your bodies shall flourish like the grass; and it shall be known that the hand of the Lord is with his servants." —Isaiah 66:14

~ PRAYERS ~

Prayer for the Cycles of Womanhood

Lord,

You have made my female body to operate in physical cycles. Sometimes those cycles bring me comfort, joy, and pleasure. Other days they bring me discomfort, pain, and irritation. Give me the grace to be thankful for the cycles that mark my womanhood, the ebb and flow of hormones and chemicals, blood and water, pleasure and discomfort that are uniquely feminine and uniquely mine in my own body. I offer every thought, feeling, physical reaction, and emotion these cycles create in me to you, recognizing their inherent goodness. Renew me when I feel overcome by the demands of my female body. Give me the presence of mind to recognize when my body's cycles are comforting and life-giving and give you thanks. I trust that as my body cycles through its natural processes, they are guided by your hand. I surrender the whole length of my days to you, O God, and with them the wonder of my womanhood. Grant me health of mind and body, bring me healing where I need it, and use this body in all its phases according to your holy will. Amen.

Prayer for When Your Mind and Emotions Are Fragile

Sweet Jesus, my incarnate Lord,

In your time on earth, you witnessed women in so many states. You watched women grieve and rejoice, weep with sadness and embrace in joy. You saw us sing and you saw us sleep. You saw us work and you saw us fail at our duties. You saw us at our best and our worst. And always, always, you reached for us in love and compassion and drew us to you. So I know that this fragility I feel today, this coming undone, all loose at my seams, I can show you. Help me, Jesus. See me, Jesus. I feel all alone. I am surrounded by so much darkness. I am afraid and wonder if anyone could possibly understand. I remember your earthly life, the way you loved the women you encountered in whatever state you found them. I remember the cross and the thorns that pierced your head and the sweat that turned to blood in your great agony, and the friends who were not there when you turned to them for help. And I know that you know, Lord. I am not sure whether to offer this unstable mind to you as gift or to ask you to heal it, but what I do know is I need to know you are near. Breathe your peace over me, and touch the depths of my humanity with your understanding. Contain me, my precious, suffering Savior, as I throw myself into your mercy, and hold the pieces of me together when I cannot. Amen.

Prayer to the Blessed Mother When You Fear You Are Not Enough

Precious Mother,

I am not a perfect woman. I am nowhere close to being a perfect woman. But I am the daughter of my Father and your daughter too. I am afraid, Mother. I am afraid that in my imperfection, I am not enough. My eyes have wandered from your loving, accepting gaze and looked out at the sea of "betterness" that surrounds me. Dearest Mother, bring me back into the peaceful embrace, the protection of your loveliness, the mantel that shields my vision of every thought of not being enough to be worthy of love. Pray for me, dear Mother, that my heart may utter with yours a complete assent to who God has called me and only me to be. And lead me by your example of praise for all God has done for me and in me. May your prayers reach the ears of your beloved on your perfectly pure and spotless lips, and may the grace he grants return to me in your hands, the loving touch of you, my Mother, bringing me back from fear to the safety of a perfect love, that is always enough and fills every space where I am lacking. Satisfy me as a child resting confidently in your arms, through the mercy of your son Jesus Christ. Amen.

Pray for Your Talitha

Heavenly Father,

I recognize that sometimes my relationship with you, my ability to trust you, to surrender my life completely to you are affected by my childhood experiences. I know that there is a little girl inside me who still hurts in many ways. And that I am still her, even as the adult woman I am today. There is a little girl who was wounded by others in ways only I know. There is a little girl who remembers the moment she went from thinking she was beautiful to knowing she was not. There is a little girl who knows what it feels like to be unwanted by someone. There is a little girl who knows the pain of rejection. And that little girl still lives in my heart, longing for your love, and at the same time putting on a defensive armor to keep from experiencing any more pain. Come into the room of my heart, Lord; see me lying there, young and small, eyes closed. Take my hand and lift me up. Call to me to arise, my *Talitha*, my precious, little one. Bring her back to life, O God, so that I may know the abundance of your love and live fully once again. Give me back my little girl, Lord, so that the woman I am may pursue holiness in wholeness. Amen.

Prayer for Weightlessness

Spirit, consoler, and advocate,

I am sinking under the expectations of the world. Always, no matter what, it seems I am too heavy for someone. My body weighs too much. My thoughts are too deep. My heart is too broken. I long to be held by someone who does not see me as too much. I long to be light and ethereal, like you when you came as a pure white dove, or dancing flames of fire, or a gentle wind across the earth. It seems I cannot be lifted out of this burden of being too much, too heavy for the world I live in. I place my trust in you, who comes to perfect my faith. I give you this heaviness and trust your love will hold all of me. I thrust myself into the spaciousness of you, the wideness of your grace, I lie back and relax in the sea of your love, and let myself be held, buoyed by your consoling hand. I am weightless in the wide ocean of mercy; grant that I may remember I am never more than you can hold and give me freedom from every spirit that weighs me down with heavier expectations than you have of me. I am yours; hold me, and restore the lightness that is mine in knowing there is room for all of me in you. Amen.

~ Meditations ~

Meditation on Your Creation

Close your eyes and picture the hands of God at work creating you. Imagine the way he moved as he layered you together, cell by cell, joint by joint. Picture the joy among the Trinity as you came into being, as your eye color was decided and the shape of your ears molded. Stay there for as long as possible, in the moment you were made into someone by the hands of God in pure and total love. Imagine him cradling your precious soul as he placed it gently inside the body he molded to house his goodness. See his Spirit overshadowing you with the protective instinct of a loving Father as you came into being. Let the images wash over you and let your heart respond earnestly and honestly to these images. Don't ask why. Don't go to the dark places. Bask in seeing the great delight on God's face as he formed you and meditate on that delight.

Meditation to Reconnect with Your Body

As you lay your head on your pillow and still your body from the day's activities, recognize the ways you have gone numb today to your body and its needs. Feel the places you are holding tension, anxiety, or the pain of failure from the day. Feel the weight of the day's sins or imperfections. Slow your breathing, and as you inhale, imagine God's love and mercy flooding your body. As you exhale, release the tensions, fears, failures and sins of the day to him. Starting at the top of your head and moving downward, simply recognize every part of your body, feel the sensation of its connectedness to the other parts of your body, and how it houses your spirit. Relax into rest, remembering that your body and soul are one, aware of their union and their combined goodness. Speak a healing prayer over any part of you—physical, spiritual, or emotional—that needs it. Wiggle your fingers rapidly, then gradually more and more slowly until they are still. Let your body follow into that stillness, and invite it into rest, offering it as gift.

Meditation on How to Care for Yourself Well

Borrowed from Jessica's story shared earlier in the book, take the time each day to think through this list in the morning and give yourself permission to respond to your own needs:

When will I take time for a warm bath or other comforting routine today? I give myself permission to seek comfort that renews and restores me, body and spirit.

How will I feed myself well today? I give myself permission to sit, to eat my meals peacefully and slowly, and to prepare myself the foods that I know nourish me well.

I need hydration to feel alert and energetic. I will remember my water today. I give myself permission to stop when I need to and keep my body filled with what it needs to perform its duties well.

Am I reacting or failing to react out of sheer tiredness? Am I feeling less than well, overly anxious, on the verge of depression? Where can I schedule extra sleep as preventative care? I give myself permission to rest when I need it.

Am I feeling alone and like no one can understand me? Am I too overwhelmed or anxious to see solutions or hope in my situation? Who can I call and ask for help? I give myself permission to ask for help when I need it.

Meditation on Your Place in the Universe

Sit outside if you can and stop to picture some of the glories of the universe. The vastness of the Milky Way. The number of stars. The grains of sand upon the earth. The way the ocean knows where to stop and the land where to begin. Every variety of flower and tree and fruit on earth. Every species of animal. Then think of the grand reality of every single person who has ever lived and will ever live on this earth. Think of how every one of those things, from the stars to the grains of sand to every hair on every head of every person who has ever existed and will ever exist, have been counted by God. Now see yourself, in the middle of that sea of faces, under the vastness of the sky, standing on the wide expanse of the earth. And picture God seeing you, pointing you out, looking at his only Son, and saying, "That one. I want that one. Will you go get her for me?" Now picture Jesus, taking his divinity and placing it into the first cells of human growth, thinking of you all the while. Picture Jesus through his whole life with you on his mind, remembering his Father's face when he looked on you and desired your salvation. Let your heart respond to Jesus's love freely and without reserve—bare yourself before him.

Meditation on Your Glorified Body

Take time to think about what your body will look like on that day of glory when it is returned to you if your hope of heaven is realized. What do you want it to look like? What would be the ultimately perfect form to fit your soul once it has seen the face of God? Think about details. Have a lightness and sense of humor about the dreams. What imperfections do you hope are washed away? What age will your body be? What features would you hope are not changed? As you think through the details of your glorified body, let the hope of heaven build inside you and offer a prayer of desirous love to God, the Lover of your soul. Look at yourself in the mirror after your meditation and smile, thinking of the way you already reflect the radiance of that glorified body, of the hope of an eternity of perfect, inexhaustible joy.

It was October when I signed a contractual agreement to write a book about faith and the female body. I was not sure exactly what that would look like, and I was not sure I was qualified to do it. But the Spirit had been pushing the questions and the concepts into and back out of my heart in words, and women had been expressing a desire for more of this conversation with great earnestness each time I did. So I agreed in faith to write his words for the hearts of women and their physical selves, to tell them of the blessing God desires their bodies to be.

I agreed even as I spiraled toward burnout, battled a yet undiagnosed mental illness, and nourished levels of self-criticism that resulted in harmful behaviors. In December, those weaknesses collided into a full physical and emotional collapse, a true nervous breakdown, requiring hospitalization and a big shift in perspective and lifestyle.

That was followed by an extensive program of therapy to recover from my bodily and mental collapse. I am still fragile and frustrated with that fragility many days. I am still identifying the roots of my wounds and the triggers that initiate my downward spirals. We are all working together, medical, psychiatric, and psychological professionals, as well as spiritual mentors, to try to figure out how to bring me back to holistic health.

And here I am, finishing this book. What I want you to know, dear reader, is that every word you have read here has been lived as it was written. I kept going because sharing this story of God's heart for women and his great desire for us to live naked and unashamed was as life-giving to me as I could hope it would be for anyone else who read it.

So I end with this note of encouragement: If you have gotten to the end of this book and feel like maybe you have more work to do than you thought when you began, that maybe you are farther away from figuring out your questions about what it means to live inside a female body at once designed by God and capable of denying him, do not despair. Do not give up hope. Do not be afraid.

I am here with you, hoping with you, believing with you, that we will be richer for having journeyed back to ourselves, for having considered who we were when we were Eve and how we are redeemed by grace. I am here with you recognizing how wonderful it is to be a woman and how very hard it can be too. And I am believing with you and begging God with you to help our unbelief.

This is not a book about getting to the end and getting it right. This is a book about walking the path of grace toward the light of eternity, back to who we were when we were Eve. And doing so together, in small and maybe uncertain steps, but always walking, knowing you are never alone. Thank you for walking with me. I hope we'll meet in the garden one day.

Sarah Margaret Babbs writes at the intersection of social justice and suffering. Having lost her mother at age seven, Sarah writes about navigating life as a motherless daughter and motherhood shaped by loss. Her blog is *Fumbling Toward Grace*. Her work has also appeared at *Blessed Is She*, *Sick Pilgrim*, and *US Catholic*. Sarah lives in Carmel, Indiana, with her husband and three children.

Margaret Baglow is a seventeen-year-old high school honors and advanced placement student, student reporter, and member of the speech and debate club. She acts in musicals and plays and is an avid reader, Netflix viewer, lover of literature and writing, and enthusiast of Nalgene water bottles and Chacos. She lives in Covington, Louisiana, with her parents and three brothers.

Elise Barrett is a mother of three, writer/editor and singer/songwriter. Her book *What Was Lost: A Christian Journey through Miscarriage* received *Christianity Today*'s Best Book Award, and she has released two solo albums. Elise is also part of a collaborative musical project called Sister|Sinjin. You can connect with her at EliseBarrett.com.

Shannon Evans is a writer, podcaster, community dweller, and appreciator of odd people. Find her online at her blog *We, A Great Parade* and on Instagram as @shannonkevans.

Jessica Mesman Griffith is the cofounder of *Sick Pilgrim*, a blog and community for artists and other spiritual misfits, and the author of four books, including the memoirs *Love and Salt* and

Strange Journey. You can find her online at JessicaMesman.com.

Judy Landrieu Klein is an author, theologian and inspirational speaker. Her books include *Miracle Man* and *Mary's Way: The Power of Entrusting Your Child to God.* Judy writes about the spiritual life at MemorareMinistries.com.

Mary Lenaburg is a writer, speaker, wife and mother sharing her witness and testimony about God's redeeming love and the faith that gives us courage to want what God wants for us, even if we cannot see where the path leads. Mary lives in Northern Virginia with her husband of twenty-eight years and her grown son. She can be found at MaryLenaburg.com.

Kim Padan hopes to help people find joy in a deeper relationship with Jesus and fuller reliance on the sacraments. She has been married for over twenty-three years, having one son, Gabriel, who was stillborn, and forty-one foster children over eight years. She blogs about life and faith at GabrielsMom.com.

Sharon Wilson lives in Minnesota with her husband, two kids and assorted animals. She speaks, writes and shares about God's healing and the great gift of being Catholic. Find her at GlorifiedWounds.com.

The Whole Human Person at a Glance

Rational Powers	Intellect	Speculative	
		Practical	Prudence
	Will (Spiritual Desire) Fully human love		Justice

Animal Powers (Emotions or Passions)	Sense Knowledge	Unifying/Common Sense		Internal
		Estimation / Useful Judgment	Instinct (Animal)	
		Memory	Recollection (Animal & Man)	
			Reminiscence (Man Only)	
		Imagination	Reproductive (Animal & Man)	
			Creative (Man Only)	
		Act of Sensation	Sight	External
			Hearing	
			Smell	
			Taste	
			Touch	
	Sense Appetite	Source of Energy	Hope	Irascible
			Courage	
			Fear — Fortitude	
			Despair	
			Anger	
		Cause of Inner Movement	Love — Toward GOOD	Concupiscible
			Desire	
			Joy — Temperance	
			Hate	
			Aversion — Away from Evil	
			Sorrow	
		Movement from place to place — Locomotive		
Vegetative Powers		Reproduction		
		Growth		
		Nutrition		

NOTES

Introduction
1. Walter Schu, and George Weigel. *The Splendor of Love: John Paul II's Vision for Marriage and Family* (New Hope, KY: New Hope, 2003), 82.

Chapter Two
2. Schu and Weigel, 81.
3. Online Etymology Dictionary, s.v. *"integrate."*

Chapter Three
4. Athanasius of Alexandria, *On the Incarnation.*

Chapter Four
5. Schu and Weigel, 65
6. Jewish Women's Archive Encyclopedia, s.v. "mikveh," by Beth Wagner, https://jwa.org/encyclopedia/article/mikveh.
7. Msgr. Charles Pope, "Five Remedies for Sorrow from Saint Thomas Aquinas," Community in Mission, http://blog.adw.org/2013/10/five-remedies-for-sorrow-from-st-thomas-aquinas/.

Chapter Six
8. West, Christopher. *Good News About Sex & Marriage: Answers to Your Honest Questions About Catholic Teaching* (Cincinnati: Servant, 2013), Bottom of Form 97.
9. Thomas Merton, *New Seeds of Contemplation* (New York: Norton, 2007).
10. Roni Caryn Rabin, "Nearly 1 in 5 Women in U.S. Survey Say They Have been Sexually Assaulted," *New York Times*, December 14, 2011.

Chapter Seven
11. Victor E. Frankl, *Man's Search for Meaning.* Boston: Beacon, 2017.

Chapter Eight
12. Micah Boyett, *Found: A Story Of Questions, Grace and Everyday Prayer* (Brentwood, TN: Worthy, 2014), 204.
13. Baker's Evangelical Dictionary of Biblical Theology, s.v. "delight," Bible Study Tools, http://www.biblestudytools.com/dictionaries/bakers-evangelical-dictionary/delight.html.
14. Emily Dickinson, 317, *The Poems of Emily Dickinson* (Cambridge, MA: Belknap, 1999), 10.

Chapter Nine
15. Online Etymology Dictionary, s.v. "consummate."
16. "The Song of Songs—Introduction," USCCB, http://www.usccb.org/bible/songofsongs/0.

About the Author

Colleen Mitchell is a wife, bringer-upper of boys, Gospel adventurer, wannabe saint, author and speaker. She is the author of the award-winning *Who Does He Say You Are: Women Transformed by Christ in the Gospels.* Her latest adventure has taken her from the jungle of Costa Rica where she and her family served as missionaries for six years, to the wilds of a sixth-grade classroom in Indiana, where she is still living her mission to give everyone she meets just a little Jesus.